PSYCHOLOGY OF MEDITATION

About the Author

S. K. Kiran Kumar is a clinical psychologist, teaching in the Department of Psychology, University of Mysore, Mysore, for the past nineteen years. He was a Fulbright Post-Doctoral Fellow at Saybrook Institute Graduate School and Research Centre, San Francisco, U.S.A. and conducted a study on cultural aspects of meditation, on which this book is based. He was a Visiting Lecturer at Bihar School of Yoga, Munger, India. He has long been involved with meditation both personally as a regular meditator, and professionally, using meditation with clients and conducting research in this area. He has delivered lectures on meditation both in U.S. as well as in India. His personal research work, presentations in conferences, seminars and workshops are on topics related to clinical psychology, consciousness, holistic health, Indian psychology, meditation, social cognition, and yoga. He has guided students at Master's and Doctoral level in some of these areas. He is also associated with different institutions as an honorary clinical psychologist/counsellor. He is a Fellow of Indian Association of Clinical Psychologists, and Member, National Academy of Psychology, India.

PSYCHOLOGY OF MEDITATION
A Contextual Approach

S. K. KIRAN KUMAR, Ph.D.
Department of Studies in Psychology
University of Mysore
Mysore-570006

CONCEPT PUBLISHING COMPANY, NEW DELHI - 110059

ISBN 81-7022-932-4

First Published 2002

Published and Printed by
Ashok Kumar Mittal
Concept Publishing Company
A/15-16, Commercial Block, Mohan Garden
New Delhi-110059 (India)
Phones: 5648039, 5649024
Fax: 091-(11)-5648053
E-mail: publishing@conceptpub.com

Preface

This book is the outcome of a study conducted by the author as Fulbright Post-Doctoral research fellow at Saybrook Institute Graduate School and Research Centre, San Francisco, U.S.A. Fetzer Foundation, Kalamzoo, Michigan funded the study after Fulbright period, under Saybrook-Fetzer award scheme. A report titled Culture, Context and Meditation submitted to Fetzer Foundation as per the conditions of the award forms the basis of this book.

The basic issue addressed in this study is whether we can understand the nature of meditation purely as a technique to achieve any goal. Investigators differ in their opinion on this issue. A second related issue is what constitutes the contextual factors for meditation practice. Third, the significance of culture as an important contextual variable in determining the nature and goals of meditation. Answers for these and other related issues were sought in the experiences and responses of a small group of subjects who participated in a meditation course of six weeks duration offered by me at San Francisco and San Leandro. The study reported here suffers from limitations in the overall design, including the sample size, thus rendering the findings inadequate to draw any generalisations. Nevertheless, the leads available from the analysis of the data are of value for future researchers in the field.

I have rewritten first three chapters wherever I found it necessary to render it into a book format. The chapter Contextual Approach to Meditation, delineates some of the arguments proposed by pioneers in the field and also further elaboration of the issues involved. The chapter Meditation: In the Indian Context is an attempt to provide an illustrative overview of the relation between the belief systems and the meditation practices. This chapter also serves as a background for understanding the role of culture in meditation practice. Further, I have noticed in my survey of literature paucity of clear delineation of the development of meditation practices in India and their framework that is useful for research. Swami Bhajanananda's series of articles on meditation in Prabuddha Bharata from which I have summarised quite a bit is an exception. I am grateful for that.

Though my role was primarily that of an investigator, circumstances forced me to become a meditation teacher. Nevertheless, I think it has not biased the data I have collected or has influenced it. This is because; first I administered whatever questionnaires I had to use for the study and then commenced the course. Then I asked the participants to maintain diary of their daily practice, which they did. Subsequently I conducted follow-up interview based on the participants' responses to the questionnaires and their entries in the diary. In all the three phases of data collection the participants had their freedom to respond the way they wanted.

If the book serves as a guidepost to others who may be interested in pursuing research on meditation, it has served its purpose. Nothing more is expected from this little contribution. Interested readers may contact the author at the address below for any discussions, clarifications, suggestions, etc.

October 2000
Mysore-570 006.

S.K. KIRAN KUMAR
e-mail : kiku@sancharnet.in

A Few Words of Thanks

Fulbright Foundation enabled me to visit United States of America and carry out this research work as a Post-Doctoral Fellow. Fetzer Foundation, Kalamazoo, Michigan came to my rescue when I had financial crunch after the Fulbright fellowship period, without which completing the work would have been very difficult. I am grateful to both of these institutions.

Just to say I thank Dr. Stanley Krippner, Professor of Psychology, Saybrook Institute Graduate School and Research Centre, San Francisco is inadequate, for the encouragement, and support I received from him as my adviser. He is an institution by himself and I always remember his humanistic approach in everything he did. Dr. David Lukoff, Professor of Psychology and Clinical Psychologist at Saybrook gave valuable suggestions in the preparation of the report, in his role as a mentor. I thank him wholeheartedly. I am also thankful to all other Faculty members and staff of Saybrook Institute, for their friendliness which made my stay at the Institute comfortable and pleasant. In particular, I thank Mrs. Joan Sugata, the kind soul, who always took care of many of my requirements within the Institute.

Life has its own mysteries. I never dreamt that I would go all the way to U.S.A., stay in a Hindu ashram, and become a meditation teacher for shortwhile. That happened because of Swami Omḳarananda and Sister Mangala of Badariḳashram, San Leandro. They encouraged me to offer course on meditation in their ashram and facilitated my research work. As an ashram guest I had the privilege of staying and interacting with them for two months, which made me understand many things about meditation and spiritual life, and also about my ownself. I am highly grateful to both of them.

My special thanks to the Ms. Nicole, Director of Yoga and Health Center, San Francisco, for permitting me to conduct meditation classes in her place.

The participants of the course deserve all the credit, but for whom I could not have obtained data and this book would not have existed. My heart felt thanks to them.

My student Ms. Archana Raj and my wife Gāyathri helped me in transcribing the tape-recorded interviews and it was a difficult job made easy by their efforts. My sincere thanks to both of them for their help. I also have to thank my wife and my son who suffered separation remaining in New York for months together and enabled me to complete the work at San Francisco. It helped to know our ownselves better and each other. I also thank all those who have helped me directly or indirectly, whom I have not mentioned individually.

I am very happy that M/s Concept Publishing Company, New Delhi, accepted to publish this book and have brought it out beautifully. I thank them sincerely.

CONTENTS

या निशाः सर्व भूतानां तस्या जार्गति संयमी ।
यस्यां जाग्रति भूतानि सा निशा पश्यतो मुनेः ।।

—*Bhagawad Geeta*, II, 69.

A restrained one (yogin) is awake in that which is night (darkness) to all the organisms.
Ever awakened ones see that darkness in which the organisms are awake.

1

MEDITATION : IN CONTEMPORARY PERIOD

Meditation and yoga are household terms today. No more they are esoteric nor are they associated only with religion and spirituality. For varieties of problem experts recommend meditation and yoga, this includes health, education, managerial, social, and even ecological. Scope of meditation and yoga ranges from simple relaxation to profound realisation. Thousands of yoga and other meditation centres have sprung all over the world. Meditation and yoga are studied and practised by millions of people in the United States alone (Walsh, 1999) and by several millions all over the world. As the homeland of yogic discipline, India's contribution for the worldwide spread of yoga is immeasurable.

Introduction of yoga and other practices in western cultures has significant cultural, religious, contemplative, and intellectual effects in the western world. Culturally they have contributed to the globalisation, which is the current trend. In the religious sphere, they have spurred both inter-religious dialogue and competition. Contemplatively they have fostered a resurgence of western meditative disciplines such as Christian contemplation, Jewish Kabalah and Islamic Sufism. Intellectually they have led to new interest in Asian psychologies and philosophies laying the foundation of new disciplines such as transpersonal psychology, sociology and anthropology that strive to integrate Asian and Western thought (Walsh, 1999). These developments have their spill over effect in Asian cultures as well. Indians and people of other Asian cultures have become more conscious of the rich treasure house in their backyard.

Not only lay people practise meditation and yoga, it has captured the imagination of scientists also. With the introduction of Transcendental Meditation, by Maharshi Mahesha Yogi in early 1960s in Western cultures, researchers from many disciplines, primarily from physiology and psychology have investigated the phenomenon of meditation. Herbert Benson and Keith Wallace conducted work on physiological correlates of Transcendental Meditation, which is the first major landmark in laboratory studies on meditation that lent some evidence for the possible fourth state of consciousness. A study on the yogic feats of Himalayan Yogi Swami Rama, at Meninger Foundation by Elmer Green and Alyce Green is another important milestone in meditation research. Thanks to these researchers, today meditation and yoga are effective ways of stress management. In psychological jargon, they are "self-regulation strategies" (Shapiro & Giber, 1978).

Self-regulation strategy primarily refers to the ways and means of controlling and directing the activity of a system by itself, which are built-in. At physiological level, self-regulation through meditation reduces the activity of the sympathetic nervous system that is crucial in causing stress and tension. It increases the dominance of the para sympathetic nervous system activity, which enhances relaxation. Jacobson's progressive muscular relaxation, biofeedback, autogenic training are some of the techniques of self-regulation. To this list is added the ancient Indian techniques like *asāna* (posture) and *prāṇāyāma* (regulation of *prāṇa* through breathing).

Meditative practices which involve sitting and chanting *mantra*, focusing on breathing, being passively aware of thought processes are also considered as self-regulation strategies which act at the mental level. Many studies have been conducted on them and the relative efficacy of these techniques have been discussed and debated (Holmes, 1984; Shapiro, 1982; Woolfolk, 1975). In terms of practical utility, meditation as a technique can be beneficial in and of itself for psychosomatic and psychological problems

(Murphy & Donovan, 1997; Shapiro & Walsh, 1984; Walsh, 1999; West, 1987).

Increased interest in meditation in western cultures was also a response to the psychedelic "challenge" of the 1960s (Carrington, 1987). This challenge is related to meditation's potential to induce alterations in consciousness, which some believe to be similar to that which psychedelic drugs bring about. Hence, they are also investigated as "altered states of consciousness" (Shapiro & Giber, 1978; Shapiro, 1983).

Study of meditative practices as altered states of consciousness primarily focused on distinguishing meditation practices and thereby induced states from clinical conditions and other techniques of altering consciousness (Barber, 1970; Kiran Kumar, 1981; Shapiro, 1983). Attempts to portray the phenomenology of meditative states (Brown, 1977; Goleman, 1977; Kornfield, 1979; Walsh, 1977, 1978) and to understand the underlying dimensions (Osis, Bokert & Carlson, 1973) were made.

Another important focus of research on meditation is to examine its psychotherapeutic and growth benefits (Ali *et al.*, 1988; Bogart, 1990). Investigators have found that meditative practices enhance psychological growth and well being. They also serve as therapeutic adjuncts both in re-educative and re-constructive therapies, besides serving as a supportive therapy technique.

From the viewpoint of modern psychology, investigations on yoga and other meditative practices are of significance in enhancing the understanding of the body-mind relationship. They have also helped in redefining the boundaries of the discipline to include hitherto neglected human phenomena viz., consciousness, as a valid subject matter (Naranjo & Ornstien, 1971; Ornstien, 1972, 1973; Osis, Bokert & Carlson, 1973; Shapiro, 1983; Tart, 1969, 1975b; Walsh, 1980).

So what are meditation and yoga? In India, often the term *dhyāna* is used equivalent to meditation in most contexts. We perceive, or refer to, a person sitting cross-legged, with closed eyes, in a peaceful and quiet environment, may be with or without some gestures of hands (*mudra*) or rosary in the hands, as doing *dhyāna* or being in *dhyāna* to be more precise. Habitually we connect it with religion and spirituality.

Yoga is another matter. For a lay person yoga means practising certain *āsana* (postures). For those who are knowledgeable yoga has many connotations and does not just limit to some postures. In astrology, it refers to alignment of a number of planets, in the same or different houses in a horoscope. In spiritual parlance, it refers to particular practices collectively referred to as *hatha yoga* or types of spiritual practices like *bhakti yoga*, *karma yoga*, *rāja yoga*, etc. As defined by Sage Patanjali,—*yogaha chitta vṛtti nirodhaha*—yoga is cessation of the modifications of the mental activities or functions. It also refers to a total life style in Patanjali's *ashtānga* yoga. In daily usage, the term yoga also refers to coincidence of events that is auspicious or desirable. Here we are interested in Yoga as a spiritual discipline that has a history of nearly 5000 years.

Meditation in contemporary psychology

However, in contemporary psychological literature meditation is a broad and generic term to include all those different connotations of yoga as a spiritual discipline. Second, the term also refers to all those spiritual practices prevalent in other traditions like Buddhism, Christianity, Jewish Kabalah, Taoism, etc. Third, it is used to refer to many other mental devices or techniques developed by researchers, for example, Clinically Standardised Meditation (Carrington, 1987). Thus the term is used as a "conglomerate word" and under this conceptual umbrella a number of "different techniques and intents" are grouped (Carrington, 1987). They include sitting quietly, relaxing, closing the eyes, breathing deliberately, focusing attention on an object or image non-analytically, observing the thought process without judging, repeating sounds mentally, rhythmic moving of the body as in Sufi dervish dance, and so on.

Naranjo and Ornstein (1971) categorise all the different meditative practices into three types viz., the way of forms (concentration, absorption, union, outer directed, Apollonian), the expressive way (freedom, transparance, surrender, inner directed, Dionysian) and the negative way (elimination, detachment, emptiness, centred, the "middle way"). Goleman (1977) groups them into two types viz., "concentration" and "opening up" meditation. Carrington (1987) distinguishes "centring" techniques from "meditation".

The conceived objectives of such practices are as follows: (i) A heightened awareness of physiological and psychological processes leading to their voluntary control. (ii) Inducing psychobiological and psychotherapeutic effects. (iii) Effecting changes in different aspects of mental functioning and personality. (iv) Inducing changes in interpersonal and social behaviour (Carrington, 1987; Johnson, 1982; Naranjo & Ornstein, 1971; Shapiro & Walsh, 1984; Walsh, 1980, 1983; West, 1987). The final aims of these practices are understood as the development of insight into the nature of mental functioning, identity, consciousness, and reality (Walsh, 1983).

Besides classification based on the underlying psychological processes meditation is also categorised based on goals. Carrington (1987) speaks of "practical" and "spiritual" meditation. Spiritual meditation is historically embedded in centuries-old religious traditions. Practical form of meditation is contemporary and frequently practised in the west. The objective of spiritual meditation is to attain spiritual development, through a process of deepening the range of the human spirit and changing the entire life of a human being. Practical meditation affects the practitioner's life in certain practical ways, without changing their lives in an essential fashion. The objective of practical meditation is to enrich the experience of the average westerner who continues to function within the framework of ordinary society. Other researchers have also referred to such distinctions (Johnson, 1982; Rao, 1989; West, 1986).

Compulsion to make such distinctions arise from the need to be theoretically and methodologically specific in examining meditation as a subject of scientific scrutiny. It has steered the course of contemporary research by allowing value choices between the two and the research strategy adopted. Majority of the published research articles and books deal with practical meditation. The effort is (a) to tease out the underlying technique from its traditional context; (b) to understand the underlying psychological mechanisms; and (c) to test its uses and benefits in a variety of life situations.

For comprehensive overviews and reviews of such studies, one can refer Murphy & Donovan (1997), Rao (1989), Shapiro & Walsh (1984), Vigne (1997), and West (1987). Understanding meditation as an integral aspect of spiritual traditions, but again in the background of modern psychological perspectives can be found in Brown, Engler & Wilber (1986), Naranjo & Ornstein (1971), Ornstein (1972), Tart (1975a, 1989), Walsh (1980a, 1999), and West (1986).

Problems and issues

Notwithstanding these demonstrated benefits and advantages of meditation practices from hundreds of research studies, many theoretical and methodological issues are controversial. Scrutiny of the general trend of meditation practice and research reveal that there are many difficulties and issues involved. One of them is researchers' greater preoccupation with practical or secular meditation and relative neglect of spiritual meditation. The following observation of Michael West, who reviewed hundreds of research articles on practical meditation, illustrate this. "Why has meditation therefore been practised for thousands of years in a variety of cultures and religious and philosophical contexts *if this is all*[1] that it accomplishes" (1986, p.250). That is, if meditation is used only for reduction of anxiety, stress, depression, etc., then the original intent and purpose are lost and West (1986) urges to go back to the original or eastern context of meditation.

Another trend is an overemphasis on practising and defining meditation as technique, thereby focusing on the operational aspect without sufficient consideration for contextual aspects. Walsh (1999) notes that in Western culture though Asian disciplines, such

1. Italics author's for emphasis.

as meditation and yoga, have significant cultural, religious, contemplative and intellectual effects, their practice and understanding of these disciplines are partial. Many practitioners use a single technique divorced from the comprehensive practices and disciplines in which it was traditionally embedded. For example, practising *āsana* or *prāṇāyama* without bothering about *yama* and *niyama*, or *prathyāhāra* and other aspects of *ashtānga yoga*. Further, Walsh (1999) is of the opinion that though such techniques in themselves are beneficial for psychosomatic and psychological problems as demonstrated by many studies (Murphy & Donovan, 1997), something vital will be lost in this piecemeal approach.

This partial approach to yoga is not limited to Western countries. It exists even in India. Now-a-days *āsana* and *prāṇāyama* are practised more as physical exercises by many, and we find many yoga competitions held just like any other athletic event.

Third, there exists a tendency to redefine meditation within the framework of existing modern psychological theories. A number of psychologists with different theoretical orientations behaviourist, constructivist, cognitive, humanistic, and psychoanalytical are actively investigating the phenomenon (Delmonte, 1987), without due consideration for the original religio-spiritual theoretical or conceptual framework. West (1987) characterises the contemporary theoretical approaches to meditation as predominantly atheoretical for this reason. The point West is arguing about is that the current approaches to meditation do not utilise effectively existing eastern psychological theories to generate intelligent methodologies, explain results, and develop theory further. He also indicates that there are appropriate western psychological theories which are more directly relevant to the concerns of meditation such as, identity and self-concept, awareness and self-awareness, interpersonal relations, and relationship between individuals and social systems which can be utilised.

The transpersonal group has been more responsive to the original context of meditation than others. These include Brown (1986), Engler (1986), Goleman (1977), Kornfield (1979), Ram Dass (1990), Shapiro (1990), Tart (1989), Walsh (1980, 1999) and

West (1986). The difference lies in their attempt to integrate the knowledge of the ancient spiritual traditions with that of modern psychology. However, even these attempts are limited in their scope because the dominant framework of modern science governs them. Thus, they may fail to take into account the logical limits of human possibilities suggested in spiritual traditions.

Consequently, there exists certain amount of conceptual and methodological confusion. Questions like whether meditation has any intrinsic goal or is everything extrinsic to it; whether meditation refers to a particular practice or to a whole set of practices; whether meditation can be defined generically or not; and what research and strategies are appropriate to study it have been raised. Rao (1989) notes that conceptual confusion stems from the failure to distinguish between meditation as a state and as a technique; a lack of adequate criteria to identify it; and from the simplistic notion that sitting quietly and chanting a mantra is qualitatively the same as practising the rigorous discipline as advocated by the classical meditative traditions. Methodologically, most experimental studies of meditation suffer from the use of the same subject designs, in which each subject is own control, and the failure to control for individual differences in personality, attitudes, expectations, training, and the length and quality of meditation of the subjects tested.

Such problems of conceptual and methodological nature, and atheoretical approaches in the psychology of meditation have originated partly due to the very complex nature of the process itself, which is an internal event. More than that the problem is also due to socio-cultural factors and paradigmatic reasons, which are interdependent and have co-determined the direction of meditation research. The western socio-cultural ethos in which majority of the studies on meditation have been carried out is widely acknowledged to be materialistic in outlook and scientific in orientation. As a natural corollary meditation is practised from a practical viewpoint to facilitate achieving material goals and is also studied with a view to effectively exploit meditation's potentials as mental technology. These compulsions led investigators to define meditation in non-cultic context free terms (Carrington, 1987; Johnson, 1982).

Need for contextual approach to meditation

Taking stock of the progress of meditation research and the course it has taken, Shapiro (1990, 1994) observes that it is possible to identify two distinct stages, and compares them to an "hourglass". "Meditation research efforts over the past several decades, and in particular the last two, have involved a narrowing of the hourglass, seeking precision and refinement. We have tried to define meditation in non-cultic, context-free terms, to explore its utility in a variety of clinical and health care settings; to document its subjective and phenomenological validity; to determine its mediating mechanisms and component parts..." (1990, p.63). This reductionistic approach in Shapiro's view was a necessary and critical stage in meditation research that yielded impressive results.

However, Shapiro believes that a stage has come in meditation research when one has to "widen the hourglass". That is, contextual aspects of meditation have to be re-considered. He states that, "meditation is never studied and/or practised in a context-free environment...there is always a specific belief system, goal and particularistic framework (whether psychological, scientific and/or spiritual) within which meditation is utilised and studied...and there is no such thing as a context-free investigation" (1990, p.99).

According to Shapiro, there are two possible consequences if one does not consciously specify the context. First, the research on meditation may become methodology driven. That is, it gets limited to the tools we have to examine. Second, without an explicit framework of values and/or psychological health, just as other behaviour strategies like biofeedback or behavioural self-control meditation may become an amoral technology to serve the often unexamined values and cultural assumptions of the larger society, as Nolan (1972) suggested. Then the culture in which the technique is used becomes by fiat the context. So he strongly holds that the premise that we can develop and study a generic context-free meditation is a chimera. Therefore, the agenda for future research according to Shapiro is to systematically articulate and study the context of meditation rather than to create a context-free study of meditation, which is impossible, in his view. In other words, he advocates a contextual approach to meditation.

2

CONTEXTUAL APPROACH TO MEDITATION

One of the primary issues debated in meditation research is whether one can understand meditation just as a technique. Johnson (1982) has argued that meditation is essentially a skill, which can be utilised to achieve any desired goal. It has no intrinsic goal as espoused in spiritual traditions. In his view meditation has become a part of spiritual traditions due to historical reasons and its full potential and areas of application require further exploration. Therefore, he asserts that there is no intrinsic goal for meditation and his aim is to free meditation from religious context. Most investigators accept this position explicitly or implicitly.

However, such assertions rise a more fundamental question. That is, can we speak of meditation as a unitary phenomenon? Contemporary literature suggests the contrary. For example, Carrington (1987) clearly distinguishes meditation from other "centring devices". She notes that because of a limitation in vocabulary, west refers to the simple psychological centring devices, which form the preliminary steps, as "meditation". "We therefore give the same name to the techniques used to produce meditation as we do to the end state itself. According to the great meditative traditions, however, the centring techniques are not meditation. They are simply means towards the goal, which is meditation" (1987, p.9). Thus, Carrington is at pains to keep the distinctions clear and hence, in order not to confuse the two, she calls all such centring techniques as "practical meditation".

Psychological centring devices, according to meditative

traditions, serve to focus the person's attention on some single point, which helps to reinstate a sense of inner balance. It is a process acting like a psychological gyroscope to stabilise the mind and body and neutralise forces which pulls attention away from the "centre" of the self (Carrington, 1987). Bhajanananda (1980 a, b, c, d & e) has dealt extensively with the differences between concentration and meditation. According to Bhajanananda (1981a), all the so-called techniques of meditation are really the techniques of fixing the mind, *dhārana*, as referred to in Patanjali's *Yoga Sūtra*. *Dhāraṇa* leads to *dhyāna* and culminates in *samādhi*.

Most contemporary researches have focused on *dhāraṇa*, the centring devices, than on *dhyāna* proper. Even studies that employ *āsana* and *prāṇāyāma*, which are preparatory in nature and help centring are also reported in scientific journals under the heading meditation. Therefore, we seem to be learning more about the means than the end state, due to the exclusive emphasis on techniques. This technique-oriented approach is a product of western ethos on the one hand, and of scientific outlook on the other.

Western societies are widely acknowledged as materialistic, as opposed to spiritual, in their outlook. In every aspect of western culture and peoples' actions, this is reflected. Active pursuit of science and technology and approaching meditation practically are both manifestation of the same underlying outlook. Carrington (1987) observes that the average westerner does not consider meditation as "a deep spiritual commitment, if they think of it as being spiritual at all" (p. 8) and usually they learn meditation to make life easier and more pleasant.

Whitehill (1980) reflects this attitude more clearly. He states: "Reading most of the books, we are left with the impression that meditation is slightly foreign, somewhat obscure — a useful technique of self-improvement or a heroically difficult spiritual life style — but rather removed from the American way of life, vaguely threatening to it, an activity that does not quite fit us/our environment" (p. xii). Therefore, he goes on to add, "I urge that we reconsider the shape and purpose of meditation when it is done in America by Americans" (p. xii). It means to become engaged in American realities, to free meditators from dependence on and fascination with exotic, often Asian, sources and teachers, and to bring the insights of meditation to bear upon some ugly and harmful features of American life. The attempt is to 'materialise' meditation than accept it, as it is, i.e., spiritual.

Kutz *et al.* (1985) state thus: "Most people find the renunciation of their own cultural roots and adoption of foreign beliefs and habits unacceptable. It is also unnecessary. It is our assertion that psychotherapy can provide one western context for the practice of meditation." (p. 7).

That scientific investigations have contributed their fair share for this process is evident from what other investigators have to say. For example, Goleman (1978), one of those who pioneered laboratory research on meditation, observes that in American culture which is rational in outlook and "where gods are dead for the most part except scientific ones", meditation research is extremely important to make it real and acceptable. As he notes, for people it is very important to know that a Harvard psychologist in a laboratory did test on meditators and learned such-and-such. Therefore, he states that laboratory research served as a "packaging strategy" to popularise meditation. However, Goleman is of the opinion that the laboratory findings are incidental, distracting, and irrelevant to real practice and purpose of meditation. For personal practice, the findings may be a hindrance because it can develop expectations as to what should happen during meditation. Second, the laboratory research may not enrich our understanding about how one ought to meditate. Goleman says that methods of meditation have been well worked out for centuries and all that one need to do is to follow them.

Observations as above indicate to us that what is being accepted and studied under the heading meditation in the west need not really throw much light on what is considered as meditation in the east. Meditation, as the methodology of eastern psychology, as a means of experiential knowledge of mind and self (West, 1986) is pushed into the background and whatever is accessible to the scientific approach of western psychology is studied. Hence, "the irony of this meeting is perhaps we have learned little about meditation and more about our methods of enquiry" (West, 1986, p.245). Thus, contemporary thrust on meditation as self-regulation and self-exploration is perceived as limiting the scope of meditation in terms of human potentialities and its original goals (Shapiro, 1991; West, 1986).

However, not all westerners and scientists have pursued meditation only from a practical viewpoint, though their number may be small. They have sought meditation with deep spiritual commitment. What does it mean and imply in terms of daily living and, for research? The spiritual traditions in both east and west have looked upon meditation as "a means for attaining a special kind of awareness thought to be the highest state of consciousness of which man is capable", which "can only be arrived at as part of a total life way of life" (Carrington 1987, p. 7). What that total way of life includes differ from one tradition to the other, as found in different cultures. It is part of the "ethnoepistemology" (Locke & Kelly, 1986) of a culture.

Ethnoepistemology of a culture refers to the "complex of beliefs, values and recipes (social, cultural, psychological, technical, etc.), which make up the knowledge and world-view of cultural members...what any cultural member knows — everyday, routine knowledge — as well as what is specifically relevant to certain roles such as shamans, mediums, healer, diviner, and so on" (Locke & Kelly, 1986, pp. 11-12). For a person of eastern cultures whose dominant world-view itself is spiritual meditation is not alien. It is an aspect of their ethnoepistemology. However, for the majority of the westerners it is not so. Consequently, many lay people in the west interested in meditation as spiritual endeavour seek such contexts in *āshram* and monasteries. Volinn (1985) in a study on the reasons why Americans join eastern meditation groups concluded as follows. In the great majority of societies, there is some built-in-way of entering the meditative state; some release from the here-and-now other than drugs or alcohol. However, American society is one of the few exceptions. Therefore, members of the New Religious Groups who join some *āshram* may have found a way of entering a meditative state. In other words, *āshram* and monasteries provide the enthnoepistemological context that is lacking in the broader social environment of the western societies.

Just as a lay person interested in meditation, not in centring devices, need appropriate ethnoepistemological context, an investigator pursuing meditation, as a spiritual endeavour also requires a supportive framework. Contemporarily more and more investigators belonging to different disciplines have recognised that knowledge development in any field is guided by certain fundamental assumptions which are often implicit in their work. There is a considerable body of literature, which delineate this issue in different phrases like cultural mentality (Sorokin, 1937), paradigm (Kuhn, 1962; Lifton, 1976), sociology of knowledge (Berger & Luckmann, 1966; Schutz, 1967), metascience (Habermas, 1968; Radnitzki, 1968); philosophical anthropology (Giorgi, 1970; Ricouer, 1970), cognitive maps (Hampden -Turner, 1981; Metzner, 1971; Wilson, 1977) and metaphors (von Eckartsberg, 1989). Arguments in favour of specifying the context of meditation research are a particular instance of this broader issue.

Among the many thinkers cited above, it is Pitrim Sorokin's analysis of socio-cultural dynamics and the notion of cultural mentality, which appear helpful in understanding meditation research. According to Sorokin (1937) there are six systems of Truth and Knowledge viz., agnosticism, empiricism, scepticism, fideism, rationalism and mysticism which underlie the outlook of people about the nature of the universe, reality and ultimate truth, in different cultures. Of these three are major viz., empiricism (truth of sense), rationalism (truth of reason) and mysticism (truth of faith). They determine three major types of cultural mentality viz., sensate, idealistic and ideational, respectively. Sensate mentality rooted in empiricism has determined the outlook of an average westerner and the scientific enterprise. Meditation is a product of ideational mentality whether in east or west. Ideational mentality has dominated the outlook of eastern cultures for a long time and thus ethnoepistemology of these cultures are developed and systematised over thousands of years. Therefore, meditation finds its context in this mentality. However, when meditation is transplanted into cultures whose outlook is predominantly determined by a sensate mentality it loses its original import and significance.

Besides cultural mentality as a primary contextual variable, there are many other factors, which determine the way meditation is approached, understood, practised and experienced. Of them, the meditation tradition or system is important. For example, West (1987) observes that meditators from Buddhist traditions, which emphasise compassion, love and equality, may be more likely to experience change in the quality of their social interactions than a prison officer practising TM to relieve work stress. Similarly, there is a significant difference between practising meditation in a therapeutic context and in a non-therapeutic context in terms of the goal (Ali *et al.*, 1988; Bogart, 1990).

Shapiro (1978) and West (1986) have also emphasised the study of the specific motivations and expectations for practising meditation, which shape the meditative experiences of individuals. According to Shapiro (1990), many pertinent research questions regarding these background factors arise. Important among them are: antecedent conditions in people's lives (of a personal, interpersonal, cosmic nature) which may be catalytic in causing them to want to learn the practice of meditation; and precise assessment of how they feel meditation might be helpful in addressing the issues like — identity/self issues, dealing with pain and suffering, seeking meaning and understanding in one's life and the cosmos, etc.

West (1986) speaks of 'meditation career history' of a practitioner as the context to understand the experiences and effects of meditation at any point of time. Meditation career refers to a practitioner's tryst with meditation ever since he or she began meditating. It involves many dimensions associated with the practice like persistence and regularity, number of meditation types tried out, whether practised in group or alone, whether received social support or lead to social conflict, whether formally learnt or developed on one's own, effortful or gentle, spiritual or sacred, advanced or novice, and reasons for meditating. Career history also includes details about meditation experience over time, the effects of meditation, significant experiences associated with meditation, changes in motivation over time for meditation. All these factors locate meditation in the context of the individual's life.

Thus, contextual approach to meditation essentially means that meditative practices, meditation experiences and effects outside meditation are determined by a number of interrelated variables which are context specific and hence, meditation cannot be understood only as an isolated technique. However, they are interrelated factors and need to be perceived holistically. Review of contemporary studies on meditation thus point out that meditation obtains its nature, meaning and significance with reference to personal, psychosocial and cultural context.

3

MEDITATION: IN THE INDIAN CONTEXT

From ancient times, the human quest to know the ultimate nature of reality, the nature of life and existence, and the nature of one's self has progressed in two distinct directions. One is religious and the other philosophical. The religious approach is rooted in revelatory experiences, and the philosophical approach depends on the free exercise of reason and thought. Hence, the distinction between the two is not in the subject matter but in the method and treatment (Munshi & Aiyer, 1955). Meditative practices are integral aspects of the religious approach and they have served as the methodologies, of directly experiencing the true nature of the universe or of reality or of one's self. They have evolved in different historical periods and in different belief contexts.

Within the Indian tradition, meditation has been a subject of deep study, research and experiment from times immemorial. A variety of meditative practices have been developed and systematised in different spiritual traditions over several centuries. Indologists have traced the development of meditative practices in the Indian tradition to the pre-Aryan period of Indian history which dates back to nearly 3000 years BC, during the time of the Indus-valley civilisation. The Siva religion existed during that period. This was an iconic religion, and formal worship of god was the existing practice. Some form of yoga practices also seems to have existed in these cults. One of the important features of these yoga practices was "concentration" aimed at "mental control". The cults, which followed the Siva religion, glorified a life of renunciation, asceticism, wandering mendicancy, and severe austerities. This has been termed the *muni-yati* tradition (Dandekar, 1981).

Besides yoga practices, other types of meditative practices known as *upasana* have been existing till date developed in the context of Vedic religion. The Vedic Aryan ideal was one of a materially secure and prosperous family life in contrast to the *muni-yati* tradition. Accordingly, the religion of Aryans, who were the founders of the Vedic tradition, had altogether different features. Their religion did not have any idol worship. The Vedic religion did not believe in a personal God. To begin with, it consisted of hymns in praise of various deities who are personifications of the different powers of nature like water, fire, wind, and the like. In addition, there were hymns which describe charms for curing diseases, prayers for long life and health, imprecations against demons, sorcerers and enemies, charms pertaining to women to secure their love etc. These prayers were recited in the performances of certain prescribed rituals, called *yajña* (sacrifices) (Dasgupta, 1927). The Vedic Aryan tradition is known as *ṛṣi* tradition (Dandekar, 1981). Thus, *muni-yati* tradition and *ṛṣi* tradition have provided different contexts for the parallel development of different types of meditative systems in India.

Muni-yati tradition and *ṛṣi* tradition seem to represent two sub-types of cultural outlook or mentality as the famous sociologist Pitrim Sorokin has described. Sorokin (1937) has characterised those cultures which believe that ultimate truth is beyond the sensory, that can be known through intuition as cultures with "ideational outlook" or with "ideational mentality". Sorokin further distinguishes the ideational outlook into 'ascetic' and 'active' types. In ascetic ideational cultures the emphasis is on minimisation of basic needs, detachment from the sensate world and from one's self, viewing both world and self as mere illusion, non-real, and non-existing. The attempt is to dissolve the sensate milieu and the individual self in the super-sensate, ultimate reality. In active ideational cultures on the other hand, there is an emphasis on transforming the social reality through active participation along the lines of spiritual reality. *Muni-yati* tradition seem to represent 'ascetic ideational' outlook and *ṛṣi* tradition 'active ideational' outlook.

Further, Sorokin has stated that in an integrated culture, the basic outlook or mentality shapes its different aspects like philosophy, religion, law, ethics, art, and science. A best illustration of this view regarding Indian culture can be found in Facets of Indian Thought (Heiman, 1964). Similarly, even meditative practices as integral aspects of religious traditions also seem to have been shaped by the two types of ideational outlook, in the Indian tradition. We can understand this by examining the historical development of meditative practices in Vedic religion.

Sacrificial Mysticism, Ṛṣi (Vedic) tradition and Upāsana

Sacrificial mysticism is the term used by Dasgupta (1927) to refer to Vedic Aryan ritualistic religion. He uses the term mysticism to mean a theory, doctrine, or view that considers reason to be incapable of discovering or of realising the nature of ultimate truth, whatever may be its nature, but at the same time believes in the certitude of some other means of arriving at it. Dasgupta has used mysticism and religion interchangeably.

Vedic Aryan *ṛṣi* tradition evolved over several centuries and underwent different phases of development. Initially Vedic Aryans lived close to nature as a part of it rather than apart from it. Therefore, various aspects of nature, its vastness and brilliance, its blessings and maledictions, and most importantly, the inexorable and subtly operating law that regulated all the manifestations dominated their religious ideology. Accordingly, their religious practices consisted of rituals aimed at harnessing the natural forces through propitiation. Their religious practices were simple in accordance with their nomadic way of life (Dandekar, 1981). Johnson (1982) has noted that Aryans who were warriors used the term yoga in Ṛg-Veda in the sense of successfully "harnessing" a horse to the chariot. He has traced the original meaning of yoga to this act, which implied acquisition, and execution of a skill. Thus, he argues the definition of meditation as derived from this original meaning of yoga relates to acquisition of mental skill.

Out of this simple, primitive, ritualistic religion arose a complex and elaborate system of sacrifices, and a new class of priests who alone could master the intricacies and complexities of the sacrificial procedure (Dandekar, 1981). The basic characteristics of this sacrificial mysticism are the following beliefs. (a) The sacrifices when performed with perfect accuracy as per the specifications and details, possess a secret, mysterious power to bring about or produce as their effect whatever we may desire either in this life or in the hereafter. (b) There is an invariable and unfailing relation between the performances of sacrifices and the occurrence of effects (the conception of an unalterable law). (c) The Vedic literature embodies nothing but a system of duties involving commands and prohibitions. (d) The Vedic system of duties demands unfailing obedience and submission. (e) The Vedas are the only source of the knowledge of ultimate truth, which is far beyond the powers of reason. (f) The truth or reality of the nature of the commands or of facts could be found in the words of the Vedas (Dasgupta, 1927).

There are two aspects involved in these beliefs. One related to the authority of the Vedas that is rooted in intuition rather than reason. Second is the belief in the causality of the happenings and the personal efficacy of one's action in obtaining the effects. As Dasgupta (1927) notes though the hymns of praise are directed at gods who are supposed to bestow benefits, it was the ritualistic performances that was considered to be the cause of showering the benefits. The goodwill or ill-will of the gods, to whom the prayers offered, was secondary to the accurate performance of sacrifices in getting the material advantages. We can understand why even today in India in performing sacrifices the priests try to be so meticulous about their rituals.

Meditative practices as mental phenomena first commenced in this background of Vedic religion. In this tradition, meditation practices are known as *upāsana*, not yoga. It is derived from the roots *upa*, 'near' and 'as', 'to sit'. Thus the word literally means "sitting near" (Bhajanananda, 1981b). *Upāsana* first appears as part of Vedic *yajña* in the *Brhāmanas*. They are auxiliary part (*angāvabaddha*) of rituals performed to gain additional merit and have no primary significance for the success of rituals (Bhajanananda, 1981a).

In the second stage of its development, *Upāsana* was used, symbolically, to replace the actual performance of rituals in the external world. The Vedic seers and sages believed that it was possible to obtain the same results through meditation instead of the actual performances of the sacrifices. For example, instead of a horse being sacrificed, it was suggested that one might imagine the universe as a cosmic horse with the dawn as the head of a horse, the sun as its eye, the wind as its life, the heaven as its back, the intervening space as its belly, the sky as its flesh and the stars as its bones. Dasgupta (1927) has termed this procedure as "substitution meditation". Gradually this aspect of substitution meditation took various forms like substituting letters of the alphabets for Brahman or some other deity, for personified nature deity, for vital functions of the body, etc., (Dasgupta, 1927).

Substitution meditation did not involve prolonged contemplation or the logical process of thinking. It was merely the simple practice of continually thinking of one entity, process, or letter as another entity or process. Development of substitution meditation implied that the mystical power also lies in thought, and the activity involved in thinking ought to be considered to be as potent a power as the activity involved in the actual performance of material sacrifices. It was this activity or mystical power that was called Brahman, which in Sanskrit means "the great" (etymologically) (Dasgupta, 1927). We should note that *upāsana* did not aim at spiritual goal in this stage of its development.

In Sanskrit, the term *upāsana* has the following meanings: service, attendance, waiting upon; engaging in, being intent on, performing, worship, respect, adoration; practice of archery; religious meditation; the sacred fire (Apte, 1970). Except the last one, all other meanings suggest a subject-object relation involving some action. *Upāsana* is 'objective' meditation. Objective meditation involves concentration of mind on an object, which may be a deity, light, sky, etc., or some qualities like love, compassion, or one's own self objectified. In *upāsana* attention is focused on the object by an effort of will (Bhajanananda, 1981a). We find *upāsana* evolving into objective meditation in the next stage in the Upanishadic period.

Upāsana in Upanishadic mysticism

When sacrificial mysticism was still in vogue, another group of ancient Indian thinkers in the same period who had contempt for sacrifices started an intellectual search for Brahman. Indologists have noted that Upanishadic thinkers belonging to *ṛṣi* tradition, were influenced very much by the native *muni-yati* tradition and its features of "otherworldliness" like austerities, asceticism, renunciation, etc. In Upanishadic mysticism, which developed over several centuries in different phases of experience and belief, the conceptualisation of ultimate reality was somewhat different. Sometimes it was felt as the great overlord, the controller, creator, ordainer, and master of all; sometimes as the blissful spiritual experience; and sometimes as the simple unity in which all duality has vanished. Yet the most important emphasis appear to be on that "ineffable experience which lies hidden in the background of all our experiences and at the same time enlivens them all" (Dasgupta, 1927, p.52).

Thus, the goal of meditative practices in the Upanishadic context was to have this ineffable experience in which the one who experiences and that which is experienced are absent. Therefore, the next stage in the development of *upāsana* is in the Upanishads, where it was no more a tool for obtaining material benefits. Neither they connected with rituals nor did they symbolically resemble them. On the other hand, they directly dealt with Brahman, the ultimate Reality.

Unlike substitution meditations directed at obtaining certain material benefits, *upāsana* in the Upanishadic period aimed at developing fine mentality through which one could be in touch with the cosmic life. However, that was not the ultimate goal. The ultimate goal was to carry one to the realm of silence. Upanishadic seers and sages were influenced by *muni-yati* tradition, where concentration practices were in vogue. Thus, the basic process involved in *upāsana* was concentration, not imagination. Second, the upanishadic texts emphasise (a) control of desires, (b) high moral elevation, and (c) meditation as necessary conditions for the realisation of Brahman. Thus, practice of *upāsana* was only an aspect of multipronged endeavour to realise the highest truth or reality (Dasgupta, 1927). Sircar (1974) describes the nature and purpose of *upāsana*: "It is psychic concentration. It is sometimes inspired by devotional feelings...It frees the mind from the subjective preoccupations and desires. It affords a great relaxation of our being from the insurgent impulses and fosters the psychic attitude which allows communion with the heart of reality" (p.227).

The use of substitution meditation which thus began as a way of obtaining material results with the activation of mystical power through thought, in the course of time became a way to know the very nature of this mystical power or Brahman. Meditating upon wind, life, fire, etc., upon meaningless letters and upon different objects also began in this context. These types of meditation are also called *upāsana* with certain prefixes indicating the object of *upāsana*. Three major types of them are distinguished *pratimopāsana* (*upāsana* on form), *namopāsana* (*upāsana* on name) and *ahamgrahopāsana* (*upāsana* on self).

The sages of the Upanishads used sun, *akāsa* (sky) *vāyu*, (wind), *jala* (water), *prāṇa*, etc., as symbols to represent Brahman and connected each of them to a certain framework of meaning, which served as spiritual formulae. Those formulae were devices to guide the mind from the symbol to Reality. These spiritual formulae were known as *vidyās*. They represented paradigms of Brahman, the ultimate Reality. Each Upanishadic teacher was known to have developed his own conceptual model of the ultimate Reality and taught it as his (her) spiritual formula, *vidyā*, to his (her) disciples. *Vidyās* are "analogical meditation"(Bhajanananda, 1981b). *Vidyās* ceased to be practised and their true inner essence and significance was soon forgotten, long before the beginning of the Christian era. This was due to the ending of the lineage of Vedic *ṛṣis* and the absence of a living tradition (Bhajanananda, 1981a). Thus, *upāsana* of the Upanishads was "symbolic meditation" (Bhajanananda, 1981b), in contrast to the "substitution meditation" of the earlier (Vedic) period.

Upanishadic sages also developed another type of meditation, 'subjective' in nature, called *nididhyāsana* or *ātma-vicāra*, which has become an integral aspect of *jñāna mārga* (path of knowledge).

Unlike *upāsana*, in *nididhyāsana* there is no focusing of consciousness or effort of will. On the other hand, it is an attempt to seek the source of consciousness, to trace one's 'I' back to its roots. *Nididhyāsana* is a process in which the ego withdraws into its original source, the *Ātman*, instead of rushing towards objects as it constantly does. *Nididhyāsana* is difficult to practise. It is possible only for a mind, which is properly sharpened through training and strengthened by continence. *Upāsana* can give the required training for the mind to proceed with *nididhyāsana* (Bhajanananda, 1981a).

The context and essential features of *upāsana*

Bhajanananda (1983) has explicated the context of *upāsana* and its essential features. (a) The fundamental assumption behind *upāsana* practices is the *vedāntic* view of reality according to which Consciousness is the basic substratum of the whole cosmos and it is not just the characteristic of the individual self. Consciousness is the Supreme Self, called Brahman, and living and non-living beings are only manifestations of this. Therefore, *upāsana* is centred on Brahman, *Brahamāśraya*, the principle of Consciousness. (b) *Upāsana* practices begin with an enquiry into the nature of the self and goes straight into the centre of one's consciousness and main concern is the transformation of self. (c) *Upāsana* is done only on some definite aspect of *saguṇa* Brahman (Brahman with characteristics), usually a god, goddess, or *Avatāra* because the procedure is based on definite metaphysical ideas regarding the nature of the deity, of the soul, and of their interrelationship. (d) *Upāsana* is practised as an undercurrent at all times and in all places, feeling the presence of God constantly even in the midst of all activities. (e) The different stages of *upāsana* represent the different degrees of transformation of the self. (f) The ultimate goal is the union of the individual self with the Supreme Self, characterised by a feeling of deep devotion. (g) It is a process of expansion of consciousness, which influences all aspects of life and integrates all experiences of life, through active participation in the divine drama of life.(h) Experience of *upāsana* is a positive sense of joy, not a mere absence of sorrow. (i) Progress is marked by the attainment of higher and greater degrees of bliss. Even *nirvikalpa samādhi*, the highest stage, is a state of highest illumination and bliss and not a state devoid of all experience.

The features delineated above clearly reflect the active ideational outlook of the *ṛṣi* tradition that had an active interest in material life and tried to spiritualise it.

Yoga mysticism and *samyama*

As noted already, some form of yoga existed from pre-Aryan period in the *muni-yati* tradition and it was associated with asceticism, withdrawal and renunciation. Since then, in the Indian culture, life of a yogin has been associated with the above aspects. It is difficult to say exactly for what reason Indian seers adopted such a lifestyle. Dasgupta (1927) observes that their desire for attaining their highest good, their true selves, was greater than what the worldly desire could offer them. Thus, they could not compromise with any other kind of desire and felt dissatisfied with the world not because the world has no pleasures to offer. The sole objective of these yogins was to become free from all kinds of bonds and extraneous determination.

Though yoga discipline existed for many centuries, it is widely accepted by scholars that it was a sage by name Patanjali who lived sometime in second century B.C., who codified all the existing theoretical and practical aspects of yoga in the form of *sūtra* (aphorism). They are known as Patanjali's *Yoga-sūtra*. Patanjali's codified system of yoga is also known as *rāja yoga* (royal yoga). It is also called *ashta-anga-yoga* (eight-fold-path). In the sequential order, the eight aspects are as follows. (1) *Yama*-general ethical precepts viz., *satya* (truth), *ahimsa* (non-violence), *asteya* (non-stealing), *aparigraha* (non-misappropriation) and *brahmacharya* (control of sensual desires). (2) *Niyama*—personal code of conduct—*sauca* (purity), *santosa* (contentment), *tapas* (austerity), *swādhyāya* (self-study) and *Ishwara pranidhāna* (surrender to the Lord). (3) *Asāna* (posture convenient for meditation). (4) *Prāṇāyāma* (breathing techniques which regulate the flow of *prāṇa*, i.e., vital energy, not just air). (5) *Prathyāhāra* (withdrawal of sense organs from external and internal stimulation). (6) *Dhāraṇa* (concentration or uninterrupted attention, like the flow of oil when it is poured - *taila dhāravat*). (7) *Dhyāna* (meditative absorption). (8) *Samādhi* (losing the empirical self-sense, shortly or for a prolonged period). *Dhārana, dhyāna* and *samādhi* are together called *samyama* in Patanjali's system of Yoga. *Samyama* represent meditation proper in this system (Bhajanananda, 1983).

According to Patanjali, proper and effective concentration and meditative absorption are possible only when one undergoes the necessary preparation through the practice of previous steps and stages. As one gains more perfection in the previous steps the latter steps, become more effective. These eight steps help to regulate (a) one's desires; (b) personal and social conduct; (c) psychophysiological and psychomotor activities; (d) fluctuation of attention and sensory involvement. All of them are aimed at facilitating the attainment of the goal of yoga as defined by Patanjali. That is, restriction of the mental modes (*yogaha chitta vṛtti nirodhaha*). Chaudhuri (1975) has classified these eight aspects into three categories of discipline viz., 'ethico-religious' (*yama, niyama*), 'psycho-physical' (*āsana, prānāyāma* and *prathyā hāra*) and 'spiritual' (*dhāraṇa, dhyāna* and *samādhi*).

Patanjali's yoga was not just a practical discipline. It had a metaphysical basis also (Dasgupta, 1930). Patanjali accepts the basic notions of *Sāṁkhya* philosophy according to which the entire universe and its activities are the result of the interaction of two fundamental principles *prakṛti* and *purusha*. *Prakṛti* refers to the principle of materiality and *Purusha* to transcendental consciousness, in this dualistic paradigm (Ajaya, 1983). Ultimate nature of man is *purusha* (transcendental consciousness), but human beings are unaware of it because of the activity of *prakṛti*. To transcend the influence of these and recover one's true nature is the goal of Yoga.

Since all our experiencing happens at the psycho-physical plane of body-mind complex which is nothing but the manifestation of the three *guṇa*, in order to overcome their influence different aspects of our personality are to be regulated by different means (i.e., through eight-fold path). This regulation will facilitate the realisation of the transcendental consciousness through the factor of illumination *sattva guṇa*. The different aspects of yoga are recommended as ways of increasing this quality. Hence, in Patanjali's system, ethical practices are no less important than the regulation of vital functions and sense functions, and concentration. In this sense, Patanjali's system of Yoga is a multipronged approach aimed at bringing about the total transformation of the person. Hence, no single aspect of the system can be exclusively identified as meditation, if one conceives meditation as related to spiritual Self-realisation (Dasgupta, 1927, 1930).

The context and essential features of *samyama*

Bhajanananda (1983) speaks of *smayama* as *prakṛtyāśraya* (nature-oriented) meditation. (a) Unlike *upāsana* whose focus is the principle of consciousness, *samyama* is centred on *prakṛti*, the unconscious (*jada*) principle. According to *Sāṁkhya-Yoga* metaphysics, *prakṛti* is the ultimate but ever-changing cause of the whole universe, including individual minds, with the selves (*purusha*) forming an independent immutable reality unaffected by the evolution and changes of *prakṛti*. (b) Therefore, the goal of meditation is the total separation of the *purusha* from *prakṛti*. (c) The emphasis of *samyama* is on the structure and function of mind and the main concern is with various mental processes. (d) Concentration practised is essentially a process of *nirodha* (suppression) and the object of concentration chosen for meditation can be any concrete form or idea or feeling, because *samyama* is not governed by a rigid conceptual framework. (e) *Samyama* is essentially an act of withdrawal, covers only a limited field of human life, the individual's own experience of concentration and restricted to time and place. It may degenerate into a form of spiritual narcissism. (f) Yogic experience is one of serenity and absence of *dukha* (sorrow). It is also characterised by absence of the experience of bliss. *Ānanda* as a spiritual experience does not enter the realm of *samyama*. (g) *Asamprajnata samadhi*, the highest in yogic discipline, is devoid of all experience. (h) *Samyama* is objective meditation.

Bhuddhism and *bhāvana*

Buddhism, which has also developed over several centuries, has incorporated many procedural elements of both *upāsana* and *samyama* that were existing in India even before Buddha was born. Buddha himself was known to have practised many of the meditative practices available to him in the course of his *sādhana* before he experienced illumination. However, Buddhism differ in its basic worldview which is *sunyāśraya,* void oriented. As per Buddhist view, everything is in a state of flux. What appears as the ultimate reality or cause is nothing but emptiness or *sunya*. The goal of all Buddhist meditative practices, called *bhāvana*, is to realise the emptiness of the self (Bhajanananda, 1983).

In Buddhism also one finds both 'objective' and 'subjective' types of meditation. *Samartha* (in Sanskrit, *samādhi*) is mental concentration and is a type of objective meditation practised in Buddhism, which leads to various kinds of mystic experiences. Tibetan Buddhists are specialists in this kind. Vipassana (in Sanskrit, *vipaśyanam*, meaning insight) is the well-known example of subjective meditation practised in Southern Buddhist tradition. It is analytic method, which involves constant mindfulness and awareness of all experiences. The goal is to understand life and enlarge one's self-awareness (Bhajanananda, 1983).

Tāntric tradition

Bhajanananda (1981b) has noted that *upāsana* underwent modifications in the post-Vedic period under the influence of tantra which probably developed few centuries after the Vedic period had ended. Tantra combined the monism of the Upanishads with the theism of the Puranas, united *dhyāna* of the yoga tradition with *upāsana*, and made independent discoveries about mantra, kundalini, etc.

Some of the important changes introduced by tāntric tradition to meditative practices in India include replacement of Vedic images of fire, sun, air, etc., with images of gods and goddesses; approach to ultimate reality indirect, rather than direct as in Vedic period; use of words with purported mystic power to produce changes in consciousness (Bhajanananda, 1981b). In the Middle Ages, under the influence of yoga and tantra new techniques of meditation were developed which have survived to this day.

Overall context of meditative practices in the Indian tradition

The brief overview of the historical development of the meditative practices in the Indian tradition should suffice to show that using the term meditation in a very restricted sense as some specific activity of the mind or body or breath is inadequate. Such equations may bring about certain specific effects and may be useful for laboratory investigation purposes, but they do not contribute much toward personal progress or toward understanding the broader aspects of such practices. Furthermore, the different contexts and types of practices also serve to show that meditative practices are not unitary but pluralistic.

Second, what they are intended to bring about also differ significantly. Therefore, the contemporary trend of lumping together a variety of practices from different systems to arrive at an abstract definition or scientific formulation may be counterproductive.

Third, Indian thinkers clearly distinguish between ordinary concentration and meditation (Bhajanananda, 1980 a, b, c, d, & e). Meditation is not just ordinary concentration. It is special type of concentration, which is the outcome of the natural inwardness or "interiority" of the mind caused by an inward pull from one's higher centre of consciousness. It is a complete reversal of the ordinary process of perception and turning the habitually outgoing mind inward to its source. Therefore, meditation is just a stage in concentration common to all spiritual paths (*sādhana*). Each *sādhana* begins in a different way, but each has a stage that corresponds to meditation. All the so-called different techniques of meditation are really techniques of *dhāraṇa* (fixing the mind). These techniques teach how to begin meditation but not how to maintain meditation (Bhajanananda, 1981a).

Fourth, as methodologies, meditative practices are guided by certain assumptions just as is the case with the empirical methods of science. According to ancient Indian psychologists, knowledge (cognition) has three aspects viz., the knower (*jñatṛ*), the known (*jñēya*) and the process of knowing (*jñāna*). Meditation is directed at the knower rather the known. Therefore, all meditative practices aim at the cognition of the ultimate nature of the knower, the Subject, rather than the nature of the Object. In other words, Subject is the object of meditative practices. Therefore, meditation is contexted in Psychologies of Self (Non-Self-Buddhism) and the goal of all such practices is to enhance self-awareness.

Fifth, the beginning phase of meditation is clearly distinguished from advanced stage of meditation. In the early stages, meditation helps to: (i) understand the working of one's mind; (ii) gain proficiency in interiorizing the mind (*pratyak prāvaṇata*); (iii) integrate personality by providing a common inner focus for, will, intellect, and emotions; and (iv) remain centred and unaffected by the trials and tribulations of the external world. In the advanced stages, when a person gains proficiency meditation becomes a direct means for spiritual experiences which is "higher meditation" (Bhajanananda, 1980a).

Sixth, in the Hindu tradition four major human motivations are distinguished. They are *kāma* (pursuit of pleasure), *artha* (pursuit of wealth), *dharma* (pursuit of right action which harmonises the personal and social good), and *moksha* (liberation). Practice of meditation is linked to *moksha* as the goal of human existence. While the *kāma*, *artha*, and *dharma* are motivations which are within the realm of psyche, *moksha* implies going beyond the realm of psyche and experiencing pure consciousness described variously, and being established in that state. That means meditation is a means to go beyond experiences in the realm of psyche. This knowledge also influences the course and progress of meditation significantly.

Related to motivation is the personality concept in Hindu tradition known as *guṇa*. In Indian philosophy, three constituent principles (*guṇa*) are fundamental for all material and mental phenomena. They are *sattva* (principle of illumination), *rajas* (principle of dynamism), and *tamas* (principle of inertia). At the mental plane *sattva* refers to qualities like being pure, selfless, calm and having freedom in action. *Rajoguṇa* refers to action orientation rooted in desire, craving, and attachment. *Tamoguṇa* refers to ignorance, inertness, negligence, indolence, confusion, and such other qualities. In any individual, one of the three may be dominant thus restricting the operation of the other two. That leads to trait like *sāttvic*, *rājasic*, or *tāmasic*. It is also possible that one of them will dominate at a particular moment or situation and characterise the behaviour at that moment, lending themselves to a classification like *sāttvic* state, *rājasic* state, and *tāmasic* state. According to Bhagavad Geeta the aim of life is not only to be free from the influence of *rajas* and *tamas*, but even from *sattva* also. It is called *guṇāteeta* state (a state beyond qualities) (Kuppuswamy, 1985). It means neither motivation nor personality traits of an individual are in effect, because both of them are rooted in the three *guṇas* which are no more operating. The ultimate aim of meditation is to achieve such a state. The tradition holds that among those who choose to meditate, only those with predominant *sāttvic* trait persist in their practices and with the continuing practice of meditation *sāttvic* characteristics gets strengthened.

Many saints and sages, who reportedly have attained the highest of meditative states as per the tradition served as models of ascetic and active ideationalism. They have been responsible for integrating meditative practices in all their diversity into daily life. This finds expression in the form of certain attitudes and values—personal, social, religious and universal. Contemporary meditative masters illustrate various aspects of meditation. All these have contributed information about the specific type of cultural background in which meditation practices do not look strange or alien.

In India, not everyone pursues a spiritual path actively. However, spiritual ideas are woven into the fabric of society in various practices, which foster the outlook and prepare the mind of an aspirant towards *sādhana*. For common people they have been simplified in order to be practised in daily life in the following ways: (i) Morning prayers; (ii) evening prayers; (iii) ritual worship; (iv) chanting mantra; (v) devotional singing (*bhajan*); (vi) listening to spiritual discourses; (vii) viewing dramatic performances having religious themes; (viii) reading books about great saints; (ix) going on pilgrimages; and (x) visiting ashrams. These are some examples of the ways the religio-mystical outlook of the culture is integrated into, the "ethos" (life ways) and "eidos" (thought ways) of the Indian masses.

All of these provide a proper perspective on the theoretical and practical aspects of meditative way of life to one who takes it seriously. In addition to such integration into the daily life, for serious spiritual seekers there have been many "faith communities" (Shapiro, 1990) which are rooted in different perspectives on the nature of Self available in the Indian context. Eastern traditions predict that meditation will bring about revolutionary changes in belief and value systems of those who meditate (West, 1987). Thus a person with a sensate outlook might become transformed and affirm faith in ideational outlook, because of a significant "peak experience" due to meditation. In this sense, meditation is a process of human transformation. In integrating such experiences into their belief systems, supportive meditation context plays a significant role.

In contrast, in modern western societies where the sensate outlook is predominant supportive context for meditation is absent. Sorokin (1937) has predicted that western society is in its last phases of the sensate era and will change to ideational outlook. The current interest in eastern spiritual traditions by many Americans may be a manifestation of such a shift in outlook. However, this interest is far from the somewhat well established background that exists for meditative practices in India. This difference can influence those who seek to meditate to a great extent, particularly their motivations, expectations, and their approach to meditation.

The objective of this study was to examine the phenomenon of meditation, in the light of cultural differences. More specifically the study focus on how differences in belief systems, values, and ways of life relate to interest in meditation, meditative experiences, and the changes attributed to meditation practices.

4

THE STUDY

The original plan was to conduct a cross-cultural study first in USA during the fellowship period and later in India. The design was a quasi-experimental investigation with provision for pre- and post-assessment of meditators on variables related to motivation and personality. The design focused on examining the interaction of cultural, organisational (faith communities), and individual factors on the experiences and outcome of meditation. With this plan data collection work commenced. Many meditation centres, Buddhist and Hindu, were contacted and co-operation of many meditators were solicited individually. Only few participants accepted to participate and even among them quite a few withdrew from the study for personal reasons. This left the investigator in lurch in terms of time, finance, and human resources since Fulbright was a time bound programme of six months. In this circumstance, the original plan underwent certain revisions.

In the changed circumstances the investigator, being a meditator himself for a long period, offered courses for the purpose of research at two different places. The participants in the course volunteered to co-operate in the study. Thus the data for this study was obtained from volunteer subjects who attended meditation courses of three-weeks duration each, conducted at Yoga and Health Centre, San Francisco and Badarikashrama (a Hindu religious organisation), San Leandro, California. What follows is an account of that course and the study.

The meditation course and the study

Sample

A month before the actual commencement of the course, announcement regarding the course was made at both the places. Five women signed up for the course at Yoga and Health Centre, San Francisco, but only three of them participated in the course. All the three were Americans. At Badarikashrama, San Leandro, the course schedule was announced along with a date for an introductory lecture on cross-cultural aspects of meditation, a week before the commencement of the course. That gave opportunity for future participants to listen to and meet the instructor in advance. Ten persons signed up for the course and only three women and three men participated in the course. Of the six, four were Indian Hindus who had migrated to America. The remaining two were Americans, one man and one woman. Among the Hindus, two were men and two were women. In total, the sample for this study consisted of nine persons, six women and three men. Their age range was 28 to 57 years, and the average age was 46.66 years. All the participants had previous experience in some form of meditation, the duration of which ranged from three months to more than ten years. Most of them were long-term meditators. Their education level ranged from Bachelor's degree to Ph.D. They belonged to different professions like teaching, engineering, business, acting, store keeping and health.

Setting

Yoga and Health Centre at San Francisco is a place where different persons come and conduct classes at different scheduled time on Hatha Yoga, massage techniques, Alexander technique, Feldenkries method and so on. There was a newspaper advertisement from this centre seeking a meditation teacher. The director of the centre had her training in yoga from teachers in the "Self-realisation Fellowship" founded by Swami Paramahamsa Yogananda. However, no specific religious or spiritual activity formed part of the activity of the centre. The room, in which the classes held did not have any kind of religious indicators or aids to meditation like images, photographs, idols, candle, lamp, incense, etc. Meditation classes were conducted in the morning.

Badarikāshrama[1] at San Leandro is a Hindu ashram and temple founded and directed by a Hindu monk. A church was located in this place before and a cross atop the building remains undisturbed. The ashram-temple contains idols of Hindu Gods and Goddesses. It has statues of Hindu saints and, ashram walls display photographs of Hindu Gods and saints, and of Jesus, Buddha, Mahatma Gandhi and other spiritual leaders. The ashram-temple caters to the needs of all those who visit it, irrespective of their religious affiliations. It also conducts inter-religious festivals. The monk who directs the ashram emphasises the path of devotion (*bhakti-yoga*) as a means of self-realisation and God-realisation. Classes were conducted here in the evening. The Director and Secretary of the Badarikāshrama were personal acquaintances and encouraged the investigator to complete the research. Hence, this place became the second location for conducting meditation course.

Method of instruction

Classes were held in both the locations twice a week and they were of an hour and thirty minutes duration. The structure of the course consisted of the following aspects: prayer, meditation proper, lecture and discussion in that order.

Prayer: In the Hindu tradition, prayer is an integral aspect of human life and, it is a way of being in touch with transcendental reality. For thousands of years it has been emphasised that one should pray just like one brushes the teeth minimum of twice a day, once in the morning and once in the evening. In India, it was a common practice to begin one's daily routine or any function or programme or occasion, whether private or public/official, with a prayer and

---

1. A branch is located at Madihalli, Turuvekere Talluk, Tumakuru District, Karnataka State, India.

this practice has persisted to this date largely. A plausible rationale for such a practice is the 'trans-personal locus of control' belief among Indians (Kiran Kumar, 1986) which affirms personal efficacy as well as the reality of a transcendental force in determining the course of life. Prayers are believed to serve the purpose of co-ordinating the personal and the transcendental forces operating in a situation so that, the outcome of an action is positive and free from impediments. Sometimes, the prayers also connote the surrender of personal ego to a transcendental force. Such prayers are either addressed to a specific deity or they may be addressed to some divine force or being, without any specific referent and carry universal significance.

A prayer that is most commonly used in yoga and meditation classes and has a transcultural meaning was chosen. The prayer was in Sanskrit language. It is as follows:

Om asatoma sadgamaya [lead me](from untruth to truth)
tamasoma jyotirgamaya (from darkness to light)
mrityorma amrutamgamaya (from death to immortality)
Om shanti, shanti, shantihi [let there be] (peace, peace, peace)

—(Author's trans.)

In the Yoga and Health Centre, all the three participants were Americans. The prayer was new to them and they were instructed to listen to the chanting carefully. After two classes, two of the three made active attempts to chant along with the instructor and learn the prayer. One participant did not show the same enthusiasm. However, all three of them asked the instructor to write down the prayer for them with meaning. They were explained the spiritual meaning and significance of the prayer. Since the significance of the prayer is universal, they were free to think of any god/divine being in which they have faith. In the other location also classes began with the same prayer and ended with it as well. The participants were explained the meaning and significance of the prayer.

Meditation: The investigator made the choice of the type of meditation on the following considerations. The investigator was more familiar with concentration type of meditation (Naranjo & Ornstein, 1971) in personal practice. Second, the investigator did not use any mantra because he was not qualified to do so in the traditional sense. Hence, the investigator decided to teach concentration on breathing in the belly region which helps the meditator to relax and is a basic requirement for advanced meditation practice.

Meditation practice essentially involved observing the expansion and contraction of the stomach. They could keep the palm on their stomach to aid concentration, if necessary. The participants learnt that proper breathing in the stomach region is essential for relaxation, which is a pre-condition for any meditation practice to become effective. The difference between breathing completely and deeply in the abdomen, and only up in the chest was explained to them. The relationship of deep abdominal breathing to the activity of the autonomic nervous system was explained. Participants sat with an erect back and shoulders kept to the sides so that there was enough scope for chest and abdomen to expand and contract. They were asked to wear loose clothes, to loosen the tie or belt they were wearing. They kept their stomach relatively empty during meditation by either taking food two hours before, or after, meditation.

The participants were instructed to let go of thoughts, without attempting to control them. After the practice period, their doubts were addressed regarding the practice. After a week of practice, asking specific questions and correcting their postures checked their meditation procedure.

Lectures and discussion: The instruction in theory included fundamental ideas from *vedāntic* teachings, Patanjali's *Ashtānga Yoga* and from scientific findings on meditation and states of consciousness. Major themes covered during the lecture and discussion period included the following:

(i) Purpose of meditation—classical and contemporary perspectives,

(ii) Meaning of self-realisation,
(iii) Role of idol worship and rituals in spirituality,
(iv) Different types of spiritual aspirants,
(v) Different types of spiritual teachers, and
(vi) Psychological preparedness required for pursuing meditation as a way of life.

The lectures provided the participants a comprehensive perspective on meditation practice.

Method of data collection

Two approaches used for data collection included the use of questionnaires and "diary-interview method" described by Zimmerman and Wieder (1977). Both the approaches yielded complementary information. Data collection involved three phases viz., in the beginning of the course (phase 1), during the course (phase 2) and after the conclusion of the course (phase 3).

Details of Phase 1

In this phase, information regarding the motivations and expectations of the meditators about the course; their belief systems; their personality; and their preferences about ways of life were collected using different questionnaires.

(i) *Motivation, Expectation and Adherence Questionnaire (Modified version)*

This instrument developed by Shapiro (1980) has two parts, one related to biographical information such as age, sex, education, occupation, religion and nationality, and the other related to meditation proper. The latter includes questions about the motivation to join a meditation course; expectations regarding the outcome; information regarding past meditation training, practice and experiences; reasons for continuing or discontinuing the practice. The questionnaire has so far served as a structured interview schedule rather than as a standardised scale. In order to get more information that is specific certain questions were added to the original questionnaire with Shapiro's approval.

(ii) *Ways to Live*

This questionnaire developed by Morris (1956) measures conceptions of the good life. It has descriptions of 13 different ways of living, each of which emphasises values promulgated by the major religious and philosophical systems. The ways are: preserve man's best achievements; cultivate independence; show sympathetic concern for others; experience festivity and solitude in alternation; act and enjoy life through group participation; constantly master changing conditions; integrate action, enjoyment and contemplation; live with wholesome, carefree enjoyment; wait in quiet receptivity; control self; meditate on the inner life; be adventurous; and let self be used by cosmic purpose. While they are not mutually exclusive, each life style may be preferred over the other.

(iii) *East-West Questionnaire*

Developed by Gilgen and Cho (1979a), the questionnaire measures the orientation of a subject regarding his/her value system and beliefs in five areas. They are (a) man and the spiritual; (b) man and nature; (c) man and society; (d) man and himself; and (e) the rationality of man. The East-West Questionnaire is developed on the assumption that by and large eastern and western cultures differ significantly in their orientation and emphasis on material and spiritual aspects of human existence. As Gilgen and Cho (1979a) have operationally defined, eastern way of thinking is rooted in non-dualistic view of reality and western outlook is rooted in dualistic view of reality. They lead to different beliefs and value orientations regarding the five areas mentioned.

Non-dualistic view of reality leads to the following specific beliefs: (1) man and nature are one; (2) the spiritual and physical are one; (3) mind and body are one; (4) man should recognise his oneness with nature, the spiritual, and the mental rather than attempt to analyse, label, categorise, manipulate, control, or consume the things of the world; (5) because of his oneness with all existence, man should feel "at home" in any place and with any person; (6) science and technology at best, create an illusion of progress; (7) enlightenment involves achieving a sense of oneness with the universal plane where all dichotomies vanish; and (8) meditation, a special state of quiet contemplation, is essential for achieving enlightenment (Gilgen & Cho, 1979a).

Dualistic view of reality leads to the following specific beliefs: (1) man has characteristics, which set him apart from nature and the spiritual; (2) man is divided into a body, a spirit, and a mind; (3) there is a personal God who is over man; (4) man must control and manipulate nature to ensure his survival; (5) rational thought and an analytic approach to problem solving should be emphasised; (6) science and technology have given us a good life and provide our main hope for an even better future; and (7) action and the competitive spirit should be rewarded (Gilgen & Cho, 1979a).

Sorokin (1937) from his socio-historical analysis of cultures has found that at any one particular period or era of a culture, a particular outlook can be the dominant worldview and alternative views remain as minority positions. Using this questionnaire investigators have found that individuals or groups of individuals in any culture may remain as minorities holding different belief and value system, not sharing the majority view (Gilgen and Cho, 1979a, 1979b, 1980, 1983).

(iv) *Personality Inventory*

Uma, Lakshmi and Parameshwaran (1972) developed the Personality Inventory based on ancient Indian conceptual classification of human nature. According to Hindu philosophy, the whole of material universe is constituted by three fundamental operative principles *sattva*, *rajas* and *tamas* which represent illumination, energy and motion, and inertia and resistance respectively. In the Hindu tradition the distinction between matter and mind is made on the basis of the predominance of one principle over the other. Whereas physical matter is predominantly characterised by *tamas*, (i.e., the principle of inertia and resistance), mind is predominantly characterised by *sattva*, i.e., the principle of illumination. Therefore, mind is regarded as subtle matter and, matter and mind are placed on a continuum rather than being dichotomised. There is no opposition between the two. Thus, human nature is explained in terms of these three fundamental constituents and, mental activities and behaviour are understood with reference to the three *guṇas*. They are considered as determiners of temperament and personality. The presence of all the three *guṇas* in different degrees lead to individual differences in personality and behaviour (Dasgupta, 1930).

Parameshwaran (1969) conceives the three *guṇas* as three independent dimensions. In the Hindu tradition, it is generally accepted that person's psychological evolution and urge towards self-realisation or god-realisation reflects in the predominance of *sāttvic* qualities. It is also widely believed that as one progresses in one's spiritual endeavour the person becomes more and more *sāttvic* in nature. Behavioural descriptions of these dimensions are provided in the section on 'findings and discussion'.

Details of phases 2 and 3

In phase 2, i.e., during the meditation course, the participants were required to maintain a diary and record information about their daily meditation experiences. The diaries were collected from the participants after the last day of the course. In phase 3, follow-up interviews to get clarifications regarding the entries in the diary were conducted, after the completion of the course with a gap of two months. Interview also sought additional information about various aspects related to meditation.

Diary-interview method

Diary-interview method, as described by Zimmerman and Wieder (1977), is an alternative technique for participant observation approach. It is especially suited for those situations where the problems of direct observation resist solution, or where further or more extended observation strains available resources. This field procedure is useful under certain circumstances as the nearest substitute for the classic pattern of observational research, when the investigator cannot make first hand observations or wishes to supplement the data already collected. The aim of diary-interview method is to produce descriptive findings tied closely to the details of daily activities.

Some of the important features of diary-interview method are as follows: (i) diary refers to an "annotated chronological record" or "log"; (ii) individuals are specifically asked by the investigator to maintain a diary over some specified period of time according to a set of instructions; (iii) diaries thus maintained are used as a basis for intensive interviewing; (iv) the information provided in the diary forms the basis for detailed and probing interview which seek to expand the reportage, and also to elicit information on the less directly observable features of the events recorded, of their meanings, their propriety, typicality, connection with other events and so on. According to the authors, when the diary materials are used to form the basis of an interview (or series of interviews) it is similar to the "life-history method" (Zimmerman & Weider, 1977).

The rationale of diary-interview method is to use the subject as a "naive performer " and as "reflective informant". As performer, the subject (i.e., meditator in this case) goes about his/her normal activities along with meditation in a natural way, "as if" the observer were not present. As informant, the subject reflects upon the events (in this case meditation practice and experiences, and associated conditions) and reports them which provide the "view from within" (Zimmerman & Wieder, 1977).

The diaries employed in this study conformed to the pattern followed by Zimmerman and Wieder (1977) in their research viz., (1) done on request, (2) prepared to a set of instructions, (3) limited to a particular period (3 weeks course period), and (4) employed as the basis of an extended interview with the diarist. The participants were instructed to record in the diary information regarding their state of mind before meditation, their experiences during meditation and after meditation period. No other instruction was given.

After going through the entries in the diaries the participants were interviewed individually to get more information and, to seek clarifications regarding the different aspects related to practice and experiences. As Zimmerman and Wieder (1977) have noted interviews are not only a process of elaboration, filling in the details omitted, they can also go beyond the particular events recorded, touching on other aspects like attitude, belief, knowledge, and experience of a more general character. In this study, interviews did cover the above aspects as related to meditation, which were the focuses of investigation.

Method of data analysis

Different approaches to analysis of data have given rise to one of the major controversies in qualitative research methodology. Investigators differ regarding the question, "how much interpretation should there be of data" (Strauss & Corbin, 1990, p.2). Investigators as summarised by Strauss and Corbin have given four possible answers. They are: (a) data should not be analysed but should be presented in such a way that the informants speak for themselves; (b) data should be accurately described in long descriptive passages, quoting from interview notes interspersed with interpretative comments; (c) data should be presented integratively by weaving descriptions, speakers' words, field note quotations, and investigators' interpretations into a rich and believable descriptive narrative; and (d) data should be used to build theory. Here the third alternative, "descriptive narrative," is chosen to analyse the data.

The data obtained from diary-interview method and Motivation, Expectation, and Adherence Questionnaire were content analysed. For content analysis, the principles of grounded theory procedures and techniques (Strauss & Corbin, 1990) were followed. The data obtained from other three questionnaires were scored and interpreted as per the manual. The obtained findings from different data sources are presented integratively by weaving descriptions, speaker's words, field note quotations and investigator's interpretations into a rich and believable descriptive narrative, as suggested by Strauss and Corbin.

The grounded theory procedures and techniques involve seven main coding procedures and other adjunctive procedures. The main coding procedures are open coding, techniques for enhancing theoretical sensitivity, axial coding, selective coding, process, the conditional matrix, and theoretical sampling. The first three procedures are recommended as sufficient for those who are primarily interested in theme analysis or concept development and not aiming at grounded theory (Strauss & Corbin, 1990). Here only the open coding procedure was utilised to arrive at basic categories of meditation and their properties.

Strauss and Corbin have defined the different terms as follows. Open coding of data refers to "the process of breaking down, examining, comparing, conceptualising and categorising data" (1990, p. 61). Open coding is done to arrive at "concepts", "categories", "properties" and "dimensions" of meditation.

Concepts refer to "conceptual labels placed on discreet happenings, events and other instances of phenomena" (1990, p.61). Conceptualising involves "taking apart an observation, a sentence, a paragraph, and giving each discrete incident, idea or event a name, something that stands for or represents a phenomenon" (*ibid.* p.63). Conceptualising the data is the first step in analysis. Category refers to grouping together of concepts so arrived at under a higher order, more abstract concept. Category "is discovered when concepts are compared, one against other, and appear to pertain to a similar phenomenon" (*ibid.* p. 61). Properties are "attributes or characteristics pertaining to a category" (*ibid.* p.61). Dimensions are "location of properties along a continuum" (*ibid.* p. 61).

The analysis attempted here uses the above principles of the grounded theory approach to arrive at major categories and their properties. Dimensional analysis is made wherever properties are easily amenable for such an understanding. The objective is to show that research on meditation can consider these multifarious aspects, and individual studies can be conducted on each one of them. In a certain sense, what is being done here is unpacking the meditation phenomenon.

5

FINDINGS, DISCUSSION AND CONCLUSIONS

Data analysis yielded three major 'categories': (1) those related to the nature of meditation practice and process (Category I); (2) those related to the role of different factors which influence meditation practice, process and experience (Category II); and (3) those related to the effects of meditation (Category III). These categories and the concepts appear to accommodate several aspects of meditation, which are examined earlier by investigators. They are referred to as 'properties' here. The categories, the concepts and the properties are presented in Table 5.1.

Table 5.1: Categories of meditation

Category I	Category II	Category III
Nature Properties	Influencing factors Properties	Effects Properties
Perceptions	Goals	Stress relief
Practice	Belief system	Attitudinal change
Process	Society	Dependency
	Faith community	
	Personality traits	
	Facilitative factors	
	Disturbing factors	

The different definitions of meditation currently available in scientific literature seem to focus on different categories. For example, Goleman's (1978) distinction between "concentration" and "opening up" meditation defined in terms of attention strategies, emphasise on the nature of meditation (Category I). Much discussion has taken place about the relation between the procedure one adopts and the experiences one undergoes during meditation (Goleman, 1978; Naranjo & Ornstein, 1971). Similarly, Carrington's (1987) distinction between "spiritual meditation" and "practical meditation", and Johnson's (1982) distinction between "intrinsic" and "extrinsic " goals are definitions which emphasise the influencing factors (Category II). Defining meditation as a means of inducing altered states of consciousness or as a self-regulation strategy (Shapiro & Giber, 1978), as relaxation response (Benson, 1975) are examples of Category III related to effects. One can suggest that the three categories represent a three-factor model of meditation. The various properties of the three categories interact with each other resulting in a variety of meditative experiences. The details of categories and their interaction are delineated below with illustrations.

Category I - Nature of meditation

Perceptions about meditation, the way one practises meditation and the process involved constitute the nature of meditation proper. There can be lot of individual variations in each one of these properties thereby providing personalised context for one's meditative experiences. A few examples will illustrate this point.

(a) *Perceptions*

Participants carry their own perceptions and expectations of meditation. Some of them are reproduced here. As they stated, meditation is:

1. A form of prayer, it is concentration on God;
2. That which enables me to see what matters each moment and not concern myself with things that do not matter;
3. A passive process;

4. A way of integrating all these active techniques, like visualisation, relaxation, biofeedback;
5. More into this world, when my life is relaxed, meditation is very lazy;
6. Only for sadhus and priests; and
7. I didn't think normal people could do meditation.

The above excerpts illustrate how people view meditation in their own unique way, which may affect their practices, experience and outcome. While some of them (1, 2, 3, 4) represent what West (1986) has called "common essence" of meditation, others (5, 6, 7) are "biases" as Tart and Young (1989) have noted. How such 'perceptions' influence the practice in one way or the other will be evident from the excerpts cited in the next section.

(b) *Practice*

The actual practice of meditation by the participant may sometimes differ from how it is actually defined and taught by a meditation teacher. Generally, it is believed that participants of a meditation course adhere strictly to the specified type of meditation taught. However, it can be a source of error as far as a researcher is concerned. The diaries and the follow-up interview of the participants in this study suggest that such assumptions need not be necessarily true. A few excerpts will illustrate the point better.

Participant A. An Indian immigrant who has been regularly practising meditation for more than a decade stated that he made variations in the procedure being taught by the investigator in the following way:

> "I practice it with some religious practice. I pray in the beginning and then I meditate with "mantra" rather than just breathing and saying Om. Om is of course a mantra, but I begin with Gāyathri and then Om and then silent Om...you didn't mention anything about *mantra*...It is my feeling that mantra brings better results than just doing breathing practice."

He added:

"I close my eyes, I concentrate and I consider there is nothing in front of me. Just as I close my eyes, I see a black screen and that is what I concentrate on. I used to earlier concentrate on certain form of God. However, I read one article about Ramakrishna (the great sage of India who lived in the last century) that his Guru said that he should not concentrate on any particular form but should use formless Brahman. Then I changed my style...I feel better because that really calms you down much faster than...trying to concentrate on a particular form of God."

It is clear that the participant did not adhere strictly to what he learnt in the course and, made changes in practice in tune with his belief system, prior knowledge and perceptions about meditation. Other Indian participants, who are also Hindus, reported that they perform prayer or worship and chant Gāyathri *mantra* in addition to concentration on breathing.

The American participants also reported that they made their own variations in the method, for one reason or another. *Participant K* (American) had found it difficult to practice regularly and hence felt frustrated about her practice. She had gone to another yoga teacher and learnt saying "affirmations", which she found helpful for her meditation practice. Her practice was totally different, which is as follows:

"I don't like focusing on my breathing. It doesn't work for me. If I focus on it, it skips through...if I forget about it and then focus on my affirmation and then I become aware of my breathing that works. But I don't find it is necessary for me to think about my breathing. It is not for me right now. Eventually I may get more into my breathing. Right now, I need to do it to kind of keep myself. I need to get a foundation, I need to feel safe, to feel peaceful, before I get to that level of breathing."

Another American *participant D* who had practised Hatha Yoga and had learnt Zen reported that he practises both *prāṇāyāma* and meditation for 15 or 20 minutes. His procedure was as follows:

"I do *prāṇāyāma* and...then I just sit quietly and tell my mind to stop. Primarily that's what I do. Stillness, stopping the thinking". Yet, another participant who had learnt some techniques of relaxation including visualisation, yoga, and biofeedback found some of these helpful for her concentration:

"There are some breathing techniques I have tried...one or two seems helpful at times; especially if I can't really concentrate or I can't seem to empty my mind which never seems to be empty...Music as a beginning to meditation will be helpful...Oftentimes yoga before meditation is very helpful to me."

Tart has emphasised that when one begins to meditate one already has some concepts about what the mind is like, what meditation is likely to do and so forth, which influence what is going to happen. Some residue of such biases remains however much one tries to reduce them, which in turn influences what one does during a meditation session (Tart & Young, 1989).

(c) *Process*

The process here refers to what actually happens during a meditation session. It does not address to varieties of experiences one might undergo. A few examples will illustrate the point better. *Participant A* who has been meditating for more than a decade described his meditative experience progressing in three identifiable "stages". He has described the stages as follows:

"In the beginning my mind will go to day to day problems...in spite of my efforts it comes in my mind. The only way I could get rid of this from my mind is by Gāyathri *japa*...first 5 or 10 minutes when mind is wavering this chanting of *mantra* helps in concentrating and getting rid of wavering thoughts. This is the first stage.

Then this silent *mantra* Om only and that helps better. By that time, I have calmed down. Then I realise my mind is suddenly becoming thoughtless by itself and my breathing becomes little bit heavier...It stays and goes...and [in] 2 or 3 minutes I will have complete calmness and again some thoughts and then again it goes...

And then a stage comes when I really stay calm. That is most pleasurable experience I have."

This participant reported that he experiences calmness at least two or three days in a week and "that happens particularly in the weekends...and one or two of working days." When asked "are there any specific states [of mind] before you sit for meditation which facilitate this kind of experience", he responded as below:

"*Japa* certainly helps it. Chanting *mantra* not any nonsense verbal repetition but which has some meaning that helps you believe you are calming down...Gāyathri *mantra* is helping that belief and that *shraddha*".

The participant reported that if there is a "break period in meditation practice...then it gets all messed up" and one has to "re-start".

Participant D, an American, when asked about his most common way of meditating, recounted the following:

"The usual is get into breathing as I begin with *prāṇāyāma*. The rhythm of the breathing settles the body down...and the body is enlivened by the *prāṇa* as you feel it begins to reach into different parts of the body. Then the consciousness becomes clear and focused...sometimes my attention is wide outside of my body. Not in my body at all. Often I struggle between being without thought and breathing. And breathing always activates the thought or often activates it and so I go back and forth between being able to be without thoughts, just clear attention and having that attention distracted by the movement of the breath. There are times when I am free from that and my attention is completely free from any activity of the body. That attention is very energetic...like a beam or sword or some piercing thing."

Participant Y (American) had written that she joined the meditation course because she wanted to integrate the techniques she had learnt already, like relaxation, visualisation, and biofeedback to her way of life. When she was asked what she meant by that her answer was as below:

"I think meditation allows me to focus...allows me to empty a number of other extraneous things that may be going on, mental things that may be going on, and then if one of these processes is helpful it will come to my mind. I don't have to sit at 4 o'clock and do relaxation, which is the original way I was taught."

It is noteworthy that participants are able to chart the course of their meditation process and recognise identifiable and consistent stages in their experiences. However, the phenomenology of meditative process varies considerably from one meditator to another. West (1986) has pointed out that, it is the uniqueness rather than the commonality of meditation experience that seems most significant in the lives of meditators. He also notes that the researchers have often viewed meditators as a homogeneous group and, this tendency has obscured the large and real differences in meditators' experiences. This observation seems to apply not only to Category I but also to Category II and III, as we will see.

The reports of the participants under Category I also show that the nature of meditation cannot be described in a simplistic way. It cannot also be understood in a either/or manner and therefore, questions like whether meditation is a state or a technique, and whether meditation refers to a particular practice or to a whole set of practices may not be answered categorically. West (1986) has attempted to understand the "meditation career histories" of a number of subjects in terms of different conceptual continua. He notes that meditators practice varied on "unimodal versus multimodal" continuum, with many long-term meditators having experience of a rich mixture of methods. Hence, it appears essential to distinguish the novice from the experienced in understanding the nature of meditation, as he did.

Category II - Factors influencing meditation

(a) *Goals*

The questions related to goals explored (i) the expectations about meditation, (ii) motivation to join the course, (iii) reasons for continuing with the practice, and (iv) reasons for taking up some practice before. These aspects could be treated as properties and they seem to be important in accounting for a person's meditative life.

The different reasons given by the participants under expectations and motivation indicate very clearly that people already have a specific objective for their meditation practice. They create a mental set and in turn can determine what they experience and the outcome.

Table 5.2 : Goals of meditation

Property 1	Property 2	Property 3
Expectations Dimensions	Motivations	Adherence
Physical:		
Relieving stress	Information gathering	Part of life
Gaining more energy	Learning new techniques	Movement towards spiritual goal
Overcoming illness		
Psychological:		
Resolving emotional conflicts		
Resolving identity problems		
Experiencing calmness		
Experiencing awareness		
Spiritual:		
God-realisation		
Self-realisation		

Two examples will illustrate this point:

1. *Experiencer*

Participant Y was an American housewife. She did not have any background in meditation neither as a child nor as an adult. She really got interested in meditation the year before she took the course with the investigator and attended some other course, which really did not end up as a meditation course, as she put it. Her interest in meditation was due to a number of experiences which she underwent for many years of a different awareness and a need "to be that part of myself attended to". She joined the course because she wanted to provide better form to a naturally occurring process that she experienced most of her life. She anticipated that learning meditation would influence her life in future by providing a reliable source of inner contact or peace.

2. *Researcher*

Mr. K was an immigrant from India. He belonged to the Hindu religion. As *Mr. K* reported, he joined the meditation course to explore different techniques in order to find common thread between all the other forms of meditation he had been doing or reading about. He expected different meditation techniques to be given so that a person can choose what he likes best or what really suits him/her. More particularly, he expected some technique to "quieten the mind when it starts to wander away". His knowledge was mostly theoretical and he observed that he has been experimenting with different techniques and he is a researcher. Not only the goals create a mental set; they appear to persist although one is exposed to a whole lot of information, which may not alter the participants' initial perceptions and expectations (Category I).

One of the questions asked of all the participants was whether or not the course they attended has effected any significant change in their reason to practice and made them more spiritually inclined. The participants reported that attending the course made them appreciate the significance of practising meditation regularly, but did not bring about any fundamental change in their goal or made them incline towards spirituality. However, one cannot ignore the possibility of the goals shifting due to some significant experience that occurs. It can also happen when one attends a course conducted by a spiritually more advanced teacher, or as the result of a long period of practice, as one participant observed.

Shapiro (1991) has reported from his study of long-term meditators that goals and effects of meditation are a function of the time and length of practice, which vary along self-regulation, self-exploration, and/or self-liberation continuum. He has also found that there is relationship between religious orientation and length of practice, expectations and effects of meditation.

(b) *Personal belief system*

The importance of belief system in meditation practice is

emphasised by many investigators. The term belief system refers in the sense in which Shapiro (1990) has made use of the term. Shapiro (1990) has enumerated ten different aspects of personal belief system in relation to meditation practice. (1) A person's belief about the ultimate nature of the universe. (2) The factors which contributed to the development of a belief system and components within that belief system. (3) Belief as an independent variable. (4) Belief as a dependent variable.(5) Intensity of beliefs. (6) Relation between beliefs and values. (7) Congruence between beliefs and behaviour or action. (8) Our attachment to our belief as well as the specific language, symbol, and form in which it is contexted. (9) How the questions of evil, duality, self-other dichotomy, non-human caused childhood disease and death, earthquakes and other natural catastrophes are addressed by those with a belief in an ultimate, unifying universe (at the deepest level of reality). (10) The potential negative implications and consequences of beliefs.

The aspects of personal belief system refer to the belief system of an individual, as distinguished from ethnoepistemology, which refers to the cultural belief system. Since ethnoepistemology of a culture contributes to the development of the personal belief system, it tends to play a significant role in meditation practice. In this study, only the participants' belief regarding the ultimate nature of the universe was considered. For this purpose the East-West Questionnaire (Gilgen & Cho, 1979) was used which tells us whether one's orientation is non-dualistic (i.e., eastern) or dualistic (i.e., western). The two outlooks lead to specific beliefs.

The scores obtained by the participants in the direction of eastern way of thinking are 53.66%, 56.41%, 59.65%, 62.71%, 67.65%, 70.21%, 80.49% and 84.66%. The average was 66.93%. This implies that the participants as a group tended to have comparatively greater scores in the eastern direction than in the western direction. Analysis of individual data sheets revealed that the four participants who scored 67.65%, 70.21%, 80.49% and 84.66% included an Indian (Hindu) (67.65%), and three Americans.

The three Americans reported that they had some significant experiences of another dimension of their self and were practising some form of meditation to come to terms with it. The two participants whose score is above 80% were long time practitioners of Zen and Gurdjieff's method. The participant who scored 70.21% was introduced to meditation just a year before she took the course with the investigator, though she had experienced a "different awareness" for many years. The other participants who obtained lesser scores were those who did not have any experience of spiritual nature and they included both Americans and Indian immigrants. The data reveals that belief in non-dualistic view of reality has significant relation with some type of spiritual experience and the dominant cultural outlook need not necessarily determine it. When a person's ethnoepistemology fails to support and provide a framework for one's experiences then, the individual has to seek it wherever it is available. The conclusions of Volinn's (1985) study already cited confirm this observation.

(c) *Culture and society*

In obtaining information on the role of culture and society, two specific factors were probed. One related to the differences between Indian society and American society, with special reference to leading a spiritual life. The other related to the advantages of being a Hindu and disadvantages of being a non-Hindu. The observations made by the participants regarding the differences between the two societies referred to the socio-cultural ethos. When it came to the contemporary life style in India, one immigrant of Indian origin noted that the situation is no different from an American life style. She stated as follows:

"When I go there [India] what I have seen is not very many practice meditation. Making money and all these things are there. As a matter of fact, more people here are interested [in meditation]. "

Then what are the specific differences or advantages and disadvantages between the two societies? All the participants agreed that there are important differences between American and Indian cultural milieu, which play a significant role for one's meditation practice. They considered the following properties as relevant discriminators between the two societies. These properties tend to vary on certain dimensions and they can account for the difference between the two cultures (Table 5.3).

Table 5.3 : Socio-Cultural Properties Related to Meditation

Properties	American society[1]	Indian society
Place of spirituality in the hierarchy of values	Least valued	Highly valued
Social acceptance of meditative practices	Neutral to rejection/ negative evaluation	Positive acceptance
Supportiveness of environment	Non-supportive	Supportive
Faith factor	Less	More
Availability of opportunities to learn meditation	Less	More
Availability of information and models	Little	Much

A few excerpts from the follow-up interview will clarify these points. One American *participant K* responded to the question relating to the spiritual aspect of life in American society as follows:

"I don't think people think about it at all...even if they believe in it they think oh yeah, yeah, I believe in that but I don't have any time for that."

Another American *participant S* put it this way:

"I think overall, there isn't much in life that supports this effort...That's the great weakness of this society now. It's not that we don't have a religion. It's that the religion doesn't offer discipline that helps people."

This participant emphasised that a structure is very important for spiritual life and American society fails to provide it. *Participant*

1. American Society tend to be more and more open to meditation over the past decade.

K dwelt on the reasons for American society being non-supportive for spiritual life and meditation practice. As she stated,

"People...expect you to do things for your health and to improve yourself. I would put that in quotes "improve yourself". Whether it is education, whether it's better job, bigger something, and meditation doesn't have tangible results that other people could measure...It would be viewed as something that's kind of not of real value because it can't be really seen, or measured, you can't wear it, you can't eat it, you can't put it on a resume!!"

American participants felt that the lack of a "spiritual" context in their society is disadvantageous in the sense that it leads to a feeling of oddness and non-acceptance. Except for one participant who stated that America is "always working against anything eternal," the others were of the view that it is largely non-supportive. Three participants noted that California is more open than any other part of the country, in this regard. All the American participants reported that they had no notion of meditation in their childhood and they came to know meditative practices only in the adult life. According to them, there is some advantage in being exposed to meditation from childhood. One of them stated it as follows:

"Oh, sure. You begin as little children. You have a life [spiritual], that being a part of life...I am 47...I am starting to meditate now. I could have done as a little child. Then I would have been way ahead. In that respect it's...I would say, it's a disadvantage."

An Indian *participant K* had the following to say:

"I think the specific factor is, right from childhood you know, you see your mother is practising, your father is practising and of course everybody does in their own way and that is the beauty of the Indian society. I think we have great freedom of choice and then you see everybody is doing it, you just get drawn to it, just like in over here, everybody is fixing the cars over here. So a person over here knows more about cars than I...Here a six years old boy knows what a carburettor is."

Questions related to being a Hindu or non-Hindu are primarily a religious matter and should appropriately go under the section "particular religious/faith community". However, they were raised in relation to culture and society because Indian society has been almost identified with Hindu religion for nearly 5000 years and they cannot be separated easily. A similar identification with technology and science characterises American society from the very beginning. Such identifications, be it with religion or with science and technology, significantly determine the characteristics of a culture and influence the overall belief system and values of large majority of individuals living in those societies. As already discussed in the section on belief system, a person can transcend such influences and differ from the majority. However, this is possible only when one has a significant personal experience of a different nature, which provides conviction for his or her unique perspective.

American and Indian participants had mixed reactions to the questions related to this issue. There was no unanimity of opinion. Those participants who considered the advantages emphasised on different factors. One Indian participant mentioned *shraddha*, as taught in Hindu tradition, as a very important factor. *Shraddha* denotes firm faith and single-minded devotion and in this context, it means having faith in the ultimate spiritual goal and a concerted effort to realise the same.

An American *participant S* saw the role of Indian society and Hindu tradition for meditative life in the following way:

"We can see that India has continued to provide teachers, the direction, the experience, the centuries of experience...I think that not being in that tradition is like having a wall between me and the divine."

(d) *Particular Religious/Faith Community*

The participants were unanimous that attending a particular faith community, like an ashram or a meditation group, plays an important role in meditation practice and experience. The properties relevant to this as indicated by the participants are presented in the table below (Table 5.4).

Table 5.4 : Properties Involved in Faith Community

Liturgic	Interactional	Environmental
Rituals conducted	Interaction between the teacher and the taught-verbal and experiential	Physical surroundings
Chanting hymns		
Singing devotional songs	Interaction between the group members—verbal and experiential	Serenity and quiet atmosphere
		Holiness attached to the place
	Sharing experiences with others	
	Group meditations	

As discussed above, religious tradition provides the necessary structure and discipline required for meditative life. In addition to that, it does contribute by "reinforcing" and "enhancing" meditation practice. For example, participants expressed the opinion that group meditations are a more enriching experience than individual meditation. One participant stated, without it I very soon forget that there is this other. Others emphasised the sharing of experiences and learning from other's experiences.

The interaction between participants can occur in an experiential way if a meditator can be sensitive to others, non-verbally. One participant expressed this as follows:

"They [some participants] were speaking so much from the brain and they couldn't feel anything and I could feel they didn't feel anything...But the religious man sitting by your side...I felt his presence very strong. I was hopeful that I could continue being around that presence."

(e) *Personality Traits*

Analysis of the data from the Personality Inventory (Uma, *et al.* 1972) based on Indian concepts partially supports the observation made in the section on 'personal belief system'. Those participants who had scored high on eastern way of thinking also tended to score high on *sāttva* scale of the questionnaire. Characterisations of *sāttvic*, rājasic and *tāmasic* personality types are available in philosophical, religious, and other literary works in the Hindu tradition and they have been part of the dialect.

A *sāttvic* person is described as one who has discriminative intellect; who is self-controlled, serene, equanimous, and steadfast; who is virtuous, generous and gentle; and who is detached and duty bound without expectations, a seeker of self and aware of the unity underlying all diversities. A *rājasic* person is one who is driven into action by passion, is restless, is struggling; who has more desires, strong likes and dislikes, and pursues sensory pleasures; who is attached to one's social roles; who lacks clear discrimination and has distorted understanding; and who is egoistic. A *tāmasic* person is depressed, lethargic, disinclined to work, negligent, undisciplined, arrogant, hostile, indecisive, ignorant, inadvertent, uncertain and dull (Uma, 1969). It is to be noted that all the three *guṇas* are present in all the individuals and it is the preponderance of one over the other which leads to the labelling of persons as *sāttvic*, *rājasic* and *tāmasic* type. According to Indian psychological perspectives, regular practice of meditation will lead to reduction in *rājasic* and *tāmasic* qualities and increase of *sāttvic* qualities (Kuppuswamy, 1985).

The Ways to Live questionnaire (Morris, 1956) did not show any consistent response tendency regarding the kind of life preferred by the participants, when compared to their scores on East-West Questionnaire and Personality Inventory. Most participants indicated least preference for those ways of life, which emphasise solitude, withdrawal, contemplation, and meditation as against an active, participating, social existence. During the follow-up interview also participants reported that they had not considered contemplative way of life directed only at self-realisation or god-realisation.

(d) *Facilitative Factors*

Participants reported a variety of conditions as facilitative properties of meditation practice, internal and external. The properties are as follows:

Table 5.5 : Facilitative factors

Internal	External
Relaxed state	Quiet and peaceful atmosphere
Satisfaction in work and enjoying the same	Lack of problems in family and work
Constant practice and persistence	Few external demands
Value attached to the goal and practice	

It is widely known that meditation leads to a relaxed state of body and mind. Then, under which condition can one consider what is widely believed as an effect of meditation as a facilitative property? One participant who use to attend the classes always in a state of tension later reported as follows:

"I can't seem to focus on breathing unless I feel safe or calm already." Continuous anxiety and tension prevented this participant from following the meditation practice and she subsequently learnt "affirmations" like "I feel safe", "I feel calm", etc., from another yoga teacher.

The "affirmations" worked as autosuggestion and relaxed her. The experience of this participant shows that intense feelings of insecurity and anxiety may actually prevent one from practising meditation, just as they would affect any other routine.

(e) *Disturbing factors*

The participants appeared to be more sensitive to what disturbed their meditation practice than what facilitated it, for they could recount the disturbing factors more.

Table 5.6 : Disturbing Factors

Internal	External
Worry	Travel
Conflicts	Work schedules
Tensions	Family commitment
Tiredness	Physical environment
Lack of discipline	Sporadic life style
Attitude towards meditation	Problems in work

It is interesting to note that for one participant meditation practice itself came in the way as a disturbing factor because her attitude towards her practice was very rigid. As she reported she took her practice very seriously and started "judging" her meditation practice. Her attitude, I think I never do it right, was nagging her leading to frustration.

Category III - Effects of meditation

The effects of meditation practice can be many and varied. As discussed already with examples, the perceptions and expectations about meditation influence the effects of meditation considerably. Similarly, other influencing properties discussed also determine the effects of meditation practice. In this study, concepts related to three major types of effects are identified, based on the reports given by the participants. They are not exhaustive and do not rule out other effects.

(a) *Stress relief*

All the participants considered stress relief as an important outcome of meditation practice. Since the sources of stress are different, what that stress relief means differed from individual to individual. A few examples illustrate this point.

Participant K was an actress by profession. Since her recognition and the sense of feeling right depends so much on her acting ability and there was so much of rejection of what she did, she had almost developed an identity crisis. She had other problems causing tensions and anxiety. She felt unsafe and insecure. So she had joined the meditation course to "get a foundation", i.e., to feel secure through knowing who she really is. Her report of the effect of practice is as follows:

"Even when I get tense now...like I am in the world like today I am much more aware of I am not what I think...Now I feel that I have lot of control whatever that word under control means."

The increased sense of self-awareness has given *participant K* greater sense of control thereby relieving of her acute stress she used to feel regarding herself/her identity. However, she did not consider stress relief as the main objective of meditation. As she stated:

"I mean relieving stress will come. That is going to be the bonus...I don't think I ever thought of it as relieving stress...I have a deep desire to know who I am. It's really strong."

(b) *Attitudinal changes*

Attitudinal change referred to by participants related to life in general, to their values, to interpersonal relations and to the situations in daily life. It varied from trivial to profound so to say. A few examples will illustrate this.

(1) I don't know whether it's attitude...so much as awareness. My response to people and to things that happened in life is definitely changing. Just the attitude in traffic. Not being rattled...that seems to be coming to me which is not, if driving in a city, that's not something that comes naturally. It's a small thing, but it is very noticeable.
(2) After I started meditation, I'm much more patient with people and I feel I'm...I make friends.
(3) I have become more tolerant of the trials...in the life and I take it more easy than I used to before and I enjoy life better than before.

(c) *Dependency*

Dependency on meditation is a phenomenon many investigators

have not looked into. Tart and Young (1989) have discussed this issue with reference to the attachment and addiction one may develop to a guru and/or drugs consumed as an aid to practice. Young notes that more often people develop needs with respect to the conditions they require to meditate, (i.e., facilitative properties discussed above), rather than around meditation itself.

In this study, two participants did report dependency on meditation. They described what they feel if they cannot spend time for meditation regularly. Their experiences indicate different degrees of psychological dependency and one could say that it varies on a dimension from low to high.

One participant was able to differentiate between "compulsion" and "discomfort" when she does not practice meditation regularly. Her experience reported below will indicate how meditation can be a part of life and become a habit.

"It seems to be not so much that I have an objective to it. It just becomes something natural I am doing. I don't feel right if I don't do it. Right is not the correct word. But I don't feel as comfortable, but not compulsive, I got to do this not that kind. It is ...peaceful. It allows me to centre, slowdown, just generally that type of thing. So I miss it if I don't do it."

The experience of another participant is quite different and it may be considered as a classic example of dependency on meditation.

"When I don't take that 45 minutes or half an hour in the morning, then life eats me up, there's nothing left in me and in a few days, I'm cross, I yell at people, I act awful and if I remember to detach myself and sit quietly for half an hour then I have some chance of not losing everything all day."

Dependency on meditation may be as counterproductive to what one hope to achieve through meditation as any other negatively influencing factor. Hence, it is necessary to caution a practitioner to maintain a modicum of detachment regarding one's own practice.

Conclusions

In summary, this study could elicit information relevant to different aspects of meditation. The three 'categories' and their 'properties' show that to understand the phenomenon of meditation only with reference to the techniques or procedures employed is too narrow and misleading an approach. A three-factor model is suggested.

Second, the data also show that meditation and the meditator cannot be really separated. The findings of the study suggest that the understanding of the phenomenon of meditation depends on the meditator, or the person, as a context. Current approaches to understand meditation primarily from the technique or goal point of view thus appear inadequate.

Third, the findings also indicate that the process of meditation is dynamic. That means as the meditator undergoes changes in one's belief system, values, expectations, and perceptions one's meditation practice changes. Hence, the phenomenon of meditation has to be approached as a dynamic process, but not as a static incident or event.

Fourth, one could easily understand that several properties discussed under the three categories interact simultaneously to determine the phenomenon. Thus, to conceptualise meditation as a univariate phenomenon may be grossly erroneous. It is, therefore, more appropriate to treat it as a multivariate phenomenon.

Fifth, from the methodological point of view it appears more advantageous to follow some variations of the participant observation method, rather than a strict experimental approach.

Sixth, longitudinal and cross-cultural studies will bring out more information on the dynamic phenomenon of meditation than any single culture, cross-sectional studies.

BIBLIOGRAPHY

Ajaya, S. (1983). Psychotherapy east and west: A unifying paradigm. Honesdale, Pennsylvania: The Himalayan International Institute of Yoga Science and Philosophy of the U.S.A.

Ali, H., Boorstein, S., Dass, R., Goldstein, J., Goleman, D., Hall, R., Kornfield, J., McDonald, M., Salzberg, S., Vaughan, F., & Walsh, R. (1988). Psychotherapy and meditation. *Inquiring Mind*, 5(1), 1-9.

Apte, V. S. (1970). *The Students' Sanskrit-English Dictionary*. Delhi: Motilal Banarasidass (2nd Edn.).

Barber, T. X. (1970). *LSD, marijuana, yoga, and hypnosis*. Chicago: Aldine Publishing Company.

Benson, H. (1975). The relaxation response. New York: Morrow.

Berger, P. & Luckman, T. H. (1966). The social construction of reality. New York: Doubleday Anchor.

Bhajanananda, S. (1980a). Concentration and meditation - I. *Prabuddha Bharata, 85*, 7, 282-288.

Bhajanananda, S. (1980b). Concentration and meditation - II. *Prabuddha Bharata, 85*, 8, 322-329.

Bhajanananda, S. (1980c). Concentration and meditation - III. *Prabuddha Bharata, 85*, 9, 362-368.

Bhajanananda, S. (1980d). Concentration and meditation - IV. *Prabuddha Bharata, 85*, 10, 402-409.

Bhajanananda, S. (1980e). Concentration and meditation - V. *Prabuddha Bharata, 85*, 11, 442-449.

Bhajanananda, S. (1981a). Types of meditation - I. *Prabuddha Bharata, 86*, 5, 202-207.

Bhajanananda, S. (1981b). Upā sana - A unified discipline. *Prabuddha Bharata, 86*, 7, 282-289.

Bhajanananda, S. (1983). Three highways of meditation. *Prabuddha Bharata, 88*, 9, 162-170.

Bogart, G. (1990). The use of meditation in psychotherapy: A review of literature. Saybrook Institute Candidacy Essay.

Brown, D. P. (1977). A model for the levels of concentration meditation. *International Journal of Clinical and Experimental Hypnosis*, *25*, 266-273.

Brown, D. P. (1986). The stages of meditation in cross-cultural perspective. In K. Wilber, J. Engler, & D. P. Brown, Transformations of consciousness: Conventional and contemplative perspectives on development (pp. 17-52). Shambala, Boston & London: New Science Library.

Brown, D. P., & Engler, J. (1980). The stages of mindfulness meditation: A validation study. *The Journal of Transpersonal Psychology, 12*, 2, 143-92.

Carrington, P. (1987). *Freedom in meditation*. Kendall Park NJ: Pace Educational Systems (3rd Edn.).

Chauduri, H. (1975). Yoga psychology. In C. T. Tart (Ed.) Transpersonal Psychologies. San Francisco: Harper & Row.

Dandekar, R. N. (1981). *Exercises in Indology*. Delhi, India: Ajanta Publishers.

Dasgupta, S. N. (1927). *Hindu mysticism*. Delhi, India: Motilal Banarasidass.

Dasgupta, S. N. (1930). *Yoga philosophy*. Delhi, India: Motilal Banarasidass.

Delmonte, M. M. (1987). Contemporary theoretical approaches to meditation. In. M. A. West (Ed.), *On the psychology of meditation*. Oxford, England: Clarendon Press.

Engler, J. (1986). Therapeutic aims in psychotherapy and meditation. In K. Wilber, J. Engler, & D. P. Brown, *Transformations of consciousness: Conventional and contemplative perspectives on development* (pp. 17-52). Shambala, Boston & London: New Science Library.

Gilgen, A. R., & Cho, J. H. (1979a). Questionnaire to measure eastern and western thought. *Psychological Reports*, *44*, 835-841.

Gilgen, A. R., & Cho, J. H. (1979b). Performance of eastern- and western-oriented College students on the value survey and ways of life scale. *Psychological Reports*, *45*, 263-268.

Gilgen, A. R., & Cho, J. H. (1980). Eastern and western perspectives in transpersonal belief systems. *Psychological Reports*, *47*, 1344-46.

Gilgen, A. R., & Cho, J. H. (1983). On the validity of the East-West Questionnaire. *Psychological Reports*, *52*, 117-118.

Giorgi, A. (1970). Psychology as a human science. New York: Harper & Row.

Goleman, D. (1977). The varieties of meditative experiences. New York: Dutton.

Goleman, D. (1978). Meditation: Aspects of research and practice. *The Journal of Transpersonal Psychology, 10(2)*, 113-133.

Habermas, J. (1968). Erkenntnis and interesse. Frankfurt: Suhrkamp Verlag.

Hampden-Turner, C. (1981). *Maps of the mind: Charts and concepts of the mind and its labyrinths*. New York: Macmillan Publishing Co.

Heiman, B. (1964). *The facets of Indian thought*. England: George Allen & Unwin Ltd.

Holmes, D. (1984). Meditation and somatic arousal. *American Psychologist, 39*, 1, 1-10.

Johnson, W. (1982). Riding the Ox home: A history of meditation from shamanism to science. Boston, MA: Beacon Press.

Kiran Kumar, S. K. (1981). A study of personality correlates in certain clinical conditions and other states suggestive of altered states of consciousness. Unpublished doctoral dissertation, Bangalore University, India.

Kiran Kumar, S. K. (1986). Are Indians trans-personal in locus of control belief? *Indian Journal of Behaviour, 10(4)*. 25-31.

Kornfield, J. (1979). Intensive insight meditation: A phenomenological study. *The Journal of Transpersonal Psychology, 11(1)*, 41-59.

Kuhn, T. (1970). *The structure of scientific revolution*. Chicago: Chicago University Press.

Kuppuswamy, B. (1985). *Elements of ancient Indian psychology*. New Delhi, India: Vikas Publishing House.

Kutz, I., Borysenko, J. Z., Benson, H. (1985). Meditation and psychotherapy: A rationale for the integration of dynamic psychotherapy, the relaxation response, and mindfulness meditation. *American Journal Psychiatry, 14*, 2, 1-8.

Lifton, R. (1971). *Maps of consciousness*. New York: Collier Books.

Locke, R. H., & Kelly, E. F. (1986). A preliminary model for the cross-cultural analysis of altered states of consciousness. Ethos.

Metzner, R. (1976). *The life of the self*. New York: Simon & Schuster.

Morris, C. (1956). *Varieties of human values*. Chicago: Chicago University Press.

Munshi, K. M., & Aiyer, N.C. (1955). *Indian inheritance*: Vol. 1, Literature, philosophy and religion. Bombay, India: Bharatiya Vidya Bhavan.

Murphy, M., & Donovan, S. (1997). The physical and psychological effects of meditation. Sausalito, CA: Institute of Noetic Sciences.

Naranjo, C., & Ornstein, R. E. (1971). On the psychology of meditation. New York: Viking Press.

Nolan, D. (1972). Freedom and dignity: "A functional analysis". *American Psychologist, 29*, 157-160.

Ornstein, R. E. (1972). The psychology of consciousness. San Francisco: W. H. Freeman & Co.

Ornstein, R. E. (1973). *The nature of human consciousness: A book of readings*. San Francisco: W. H. Freeman & Co.

Osis, K., Bokert, E. & Carlson, M. L. (1973). Dimensions of the meditative experience. *The Journal of Transpersonal Psychology, 5*, 2, 109-135.

Parameshwaran, E. G. (1969). Indian psychology—the need for a breakthrough, an attempt. *Research Bulletin*, No. 5, 75-80.

Radnitzki, G. (1968). Contemporary schools of metascience. Göteborg: Akademiforlaget.

Rama Dass, (1990). *Journey of awakening: A meditator's guide book*. New York: Bantam Books.

Rao, K. R. (1989). Meditation: Sacred and secular - A review and assessment of some recent research. *Journal of the Indian Academy of Applied Psychology, 15(2)*, 51-74.

Ricouer, P. (1970). *Freud*. New Haven: Yale University Press.

Schutz, A. (1967). The phenomenology of the social world. Evanston, Ill.: Northwestern University Press.

Shapiro, D. H. (1978). Meditation: Aspects of research and practice. *The Journal of Transpersonal Psychology*, 10(2), 113-133.

Shapiro, D. H. (1980). Meditation: Self-regulation strategy and altered states of consciousness. New York: Aldine.

Shapiro, D. H. (1982). Overview: Clinical and physiological comparison of meditation with other self-control strategies. *American Journal of Psychiatry, 139*, 3, 267-274.

Shapiro, D. H. (1990). Meditation, self-control, and control by a benevolent other: Issues of content and context. In Maurits G.

T. Kwee (Ed.) *Psychotherapy, meditation, and health: A cognitive-behavioural perspective* (pp. 67-121). London/The Hague: East-West Publications.

Shapiro, D. H. (1991). Meditation as a technique for enhancing self-regulation, self-exploration, and self-liberation-compassionate service: A retrospective and prospective study of long-term meditators. (Manuscript received from the author).

Shapiro, D. H. (1994). Examining the content and context of meditation: A challenge of psychology in the areas of stress management, psychotherapy, and religion/values. *Journal of Humanistic Psychology, 34*, 4, 101-135.

Shapiro, D. H., & Giber, D. (1978). Meditation and psychotherapeutic effects. *Archives of General Psychiatry, 35*, 294-302.

Shapiro, D. H., & Walsh, R. (Eds.) (1984). *Meditation: Classic and contemporary perspectives*. New York: Aldine.

Sircar, M. (1974). *Hindu mysticism: According to upanisads*. New Delhi, India: Orient Books Reprint Corporation.

Sorokin, P. (1937). Social and cultural dynamics: Vol. 1. Fluctuations of forms of art. London: Allen & Unwin.

Strauss, A. & Corbin, J. (1990). Basics of qualitative research: Grounded theory procedure and techniques. Newbury Park, CA: Sage Publications.

Tart, C. T. (1969). Altered states of consciousness. New York: Wiley.

Tart, C. T. (1975a). *Transpersonal psychologies*. San Francisco: Harper & Row.

Tart, C. T. (1975b). *States of consciousness*. New York: Dutton.

Tart, C. T. (1989). *Open mind, discriminating mind: Reflections on human possibilities*. San Francisco: Harper & Row.

Tart, C. T., & Young, S. (1989). Meditation and psychology: A dialogue. In C. T. Tart. *Open mind, discriminating mind: Reflections of human possibilities*. San Francisco: Harper & Row.

Uma, K. (1969). Construction of a personality inventory based on doctrine of three gunas. Master' dissertation, Osmania University, India.

Uma, K., Lakshmi, Y. S., & Parameshwaran, E. G. (1971). Construction of a personality inventory based on doctrine of three gunas. *Research Bulletin*, No. 6, 49-58.

Vigne, J. (1997). Meditation and mental health. *Indian Journal of Clinical Psychology*, 24, 1, 46-51.

Volinn, E. (1985). Eastern meditation groups: Why join? *Sociological Analysis*, 46, 2, 147-156.

Von Eckartsberg, R. (1989). Maps of the mind: The cartography of consciousness. In R. S. Valle & R. von Eckartsberg (Eds.). *Metaphors of consciousness*. New York: Plenum Press, 1989.

Walsh, R. (1977). Initial meditative experiences: Part I. *The Journal of Transpersonal Psychology*, 9(2), 151-192.

Walsh, R. (1978). Initial meditative experiences: Part II. *The Journal of Transpersonal Psychology*, 10(1), 1-28.

Walsh, R. (1980). The consciousness disciplines and the behavioural sciences. *American Journal of Psychiatry*, 137, 663-673.

Walsh, R. (1983). Meditation practice and research. *Journal of Humanistic Psychology*, 23(1), 18-50.

Walsh, R. (1999). Asian contemplative disciplines: Common practices, clinical applications, and research findings. *The Journal of Transpersonal Psychology*, 31, 2, 83-107.

West, M. A. (1986). Meditation: Psychology and human experience. In G. L. Claxton (Ed.), *Beyond Therapy: The impact of eastern religions on psychological theory and practice* (pp. 244-267). London: Wisdom Publications.

West, M. A. (1987). Meditation: Magic, myth and mystery. In. M. A. West (Ed.), *On the psychology of meditation*. Oxford, England: Clarendon Press.

Whitehill, J. (1980). Enter the quiet: Everyone's way to meditation.

Wilson, R. A. (1977). *Cosmic trigger*. New York: Pocket Books.

Wilber, K., Engler, J., & Brown, D. P. (1986). *Transformations of consciousness: Conventional and contemplative perspectives on development*. Shambala, Boston & London: New Science Library.

Zimmerman, D. H., & Wieder, L.D. (1977). The diary: Diary-interview method. *Urban Life, 5(4)*, 479-498.

INDEX